Y0-ABO-492

By courtesy of the British Museum

From the engraving by R. Woodman, after
the painting made in 1847 by Sir W. C. Ross.

THE ART OF
NEWMAN'S *APOLOGIA*

BY

WALTER E. HOUGHTON

ARCHON BOOKS

1970

OF BETHANY LIBRARY
AN COLLEGE
CALIFORNIA

BX
4705
,N5
A38
1970

Copyright, 1945, by Yale University Press
Reprinted 1970 with permission
in an unaltered and unabridged edition

ISBN: 0-208-00954-X
[Reproduced from a copy in the Yale University Library]
Library of Congress Catalog Card Number: 78-120369
Printed in the United States of America

TO

E. L. H.

ACKNOWLEDGMENTS

THE FOLLOWING publishers have courteously granted me permission to quote from their publications: Henry Holt and Company from *Selections from Newman,* edited by Lewis E. Gates; Longmans, Green and Company from Wilfrid Ward's *The Life of Cardinal Newman,* and *A Newman Treasury,* edited by C. F. Harrold; The Macmillan Company from William Butler Yeats's *Autobiography* and *Henry Sidgwick, A Memoir* by A.S. and E.M.S.; The Oxford Press from *Further Letters of Gerard Manley Hopkins,* edited by C. C. Abbott.

I wish to thank my wife, Esther Lowrey Rhoads Houghton, for the hours she has spent reading both the manuscript and the proofs, and for her valuable suggestions.

I am very grateful to the Wellesley College Committee on Publications, and especially to its Chairman, Dean Ella Keats Whiting, for the time and effort they have devoted to this book, and to the Alumnae of Wellesley College for their generous help in making its publication possible.

W. E. H.

Wellesley, Massachusetts
August 15, 1945

INTRODUCTION

ALTHOUGH the *Apologia Pro Vita Sua* has been widely discussed, its qualities as a work of art remain partly unrecognized and largely unexplored. Unrecognized because attention has been fastened, for the most part, upon its historical and controversial aspects: on its history of the Oxford Movement, or on its presentation of Protestant, Anglican, and Roman theology with their respective points of conflict, or in the early years on the pros and cons of the Kingsley controversy. Unexplored because criticism of prose, lagging as it does far behind that of poetry, has been content with general praise for Newman's powers of self-analysis, and general references to the urbanity, clarity, and tonal beauty of his style, or vague listing of such stylistic devices as homely diction, wit and epigram, or the "subtle music of his cadences." If assertion is not to be substituted for criticism, or criticism to blink its analytical function, we need to examine Newman's theory and practice of autobiography in some detail.

The theory can best be approached by asking what equipment he had for such a work. What principles of biography were already in his mind, whether explicit or, equally important, implicit in other fields of his thinking? What kind of life story would his particular habits of character and personality, or his theories of psychological analysis, be likely to mold? What conceptions of style did he have and how might they serve his purpose? Such questions, which are the subject of Part I, are by no means biographical alone. They are also critical because they furnish a series of perspectives from which to see the *Apologia*, and, by doing so, they widen our perceptions. But to gain these advantages and to grasp the kind and quality of revelation which Newman conveys we must go on to examine the text closely, in Part II, in order to study his analytic method in action, his control of form and style in recreating the experience of the past, and his emphasis and expression as they have been affected by the aim of writing an apology. If we explore the book along these various lines, we shall see more deeply into its meaning, and we may then, in Part III, be able to estimate its success with some confidence.

CONTENTS

PART ONE

EQUIPMENT

I THE OCCASION

IT is sometimes thought that we owe the *Apologia* to a lucky accident. This is true, though the nature of the accident has been misconceived. Kingsley's double-barreled attack on Roman Catholics in general and on Newman in particular provided an opportunity, long awaited, for Newman to defend the Catholic priesthood and his own conduct from those imputations of deceit so long nourished by British Protestantism against the first, and so violently let loose against himself by the "shocking" event of 1845. At that time, with public feelings running high, he had realized that any personal defence would be useless, and had therefore decided to wait patiently until, at some future day, when old excitements had died down, some chance attack might furnish "an opportunity of pleading my cause . . . with a fair prospect of an impartial hearing." [1] The phrasing should be noticed. Pleading his cause hardly meant, I think, writing his life, but simply refuting the current charges of deceit and explaining the arguments by which he was finally converted. Certainly there is no definite evidence that an autobiography, let alone an apologia, had ever entered Newman's mind before 1864. Indeed, in the years just previous when he was collecting and arranging his letters, he was thinking of their use only by a literary executor.[2]

Then came Kingsley's notorious slander of December,

1. *Newman's Apologia pro Vita Sua,* Wilfrid Ward, ed. (1913), p. 484, from the preface to the 1865 edition. All references in my text are to the Ward edition and follow the revised text of 1865 (see Ward's note, p. xxxi). This book is hereafter referred to as *Apologia.*

2. Wilfrid Ward, *The Life of John Henry Cardinal Newman* (1913 ed., 2 vols.), II, 315–316. This book is hereafter referred to as Ward, *Life.*

1863, amplified presently in his pamphlet by accusations of "blind superstition" and "cunning equivocation." [3] Here at long last was the opening Newman had waited for, and he seized it at once. But his method of defence was not the method he had expected to use when the opportunity came. He did not defend himself by logical rebuttal of the charges, point by point, or by logical exposition of Catholic doctrine and practice. He wrote his life. That was due to the unexpected turn which the controversy took in March, 1864, upon the publication of Kingsley's pamphlet, "What, Then, Does Dr. Newman Mean?" In that pamphlet the British public was presented with the picture of a man, shuffling, superstitious, casuistical, and therefore scarcely to be trusted, however well he might argue. Newman decided that the only possible answer was the contrasting picture of himself as he was.

When first I read the Pamphlet of Accusation, I almost despaired of meeting effectively such a heap of misrepresentation and such a vehemence of animosity . . . . He called me a *liar*, —a simple, a broad, an intelligible, to the English public a plausible arraignment; but for me, to answer in detail charge one by reason one, and charge two by reason two, and charge three by reason three, and so to proceed through the whole string both of accusations and replies, each of which was to be independent of the rest, this would be certainly labour lost as regards any effective result. What I needed was a corresponding antagonist unity in my defence, and where was that to be found? . . . *I reflected, and I saw a way out of my perplexity.*

Yes, I said to myself, his very question is about my *meaning*; "What does Dr. Newman mean?" *It pointed in the very same direction as that into which my musings had turned me already.* He asks what I *mean*; not about my words, not about

3. *Apologia*, pp. 53, 58.

my arguments, not about my actions, as his ultimate point, but about that living intelligence, by which I write, and argue, and act. He asks about my Mind and its Beliefs and its Sentiments ; and he shall be answered. . . .

My perplexity did not last half an hour. I recognized what I had to do, though I shrank from both the task and the exposure which it would entail. I must, I said, give the true key to my whole life ; *I must show what I am, that it may be seen what I am not, and that the phantom may be extinguished which gibbers instead of me.* . . . I will indeed answer his charges and criticisms on me one by one [in the Appendix] lest any one should say that they are unanswerable, but such a work shall not be the scope nor the substance of my reply.[4]

Yet it was just such a work which, I suggest, Newman had always thought of as the scope and substance of his reply—until, shortly after Kingsley's original imputation of untruthfulness, the notion of defending himself by an "apologia pro vita sua" first entered his mind. It was, we see, *before* he read the pamphlet that his own musings had turned him in the very same direction, that is to say, toward an account of his own life. But at that stage the idea was inchoate and unconsidered. It was only in the half hour or so *after* reading the pamphlet, with its scurrilous attack on his character, that the actual plan of the *Apologia* took concrete shape. Years later he put his finger squarely on the crucial point when he spoke of Kingsley having been "accidentally the instrument, in the good Providence of God, by whom I had an opportunity given me . . . *of vindicating my character and conduct* in my 'Apologia.' " [5]

Thus it was that a polemic accidentally led to a biog-

4. *Idem,* pp. 97–99. The italics are mine, except for "liar," "meaning," and "mean."

5. Ward, *Life,* II, 46. The italics are mine.

raphy—and of a particular kind. Newman's own statements are needed to grasp his exact intention:

> He asks what I *mean;* not about my words, not about my arguments, not about my actions, as his ultimate point, but about *that living intelligence,* by which I write, and argue, and act. He asks about my Mind and its Beliefs and its Sentiments . . .
>
> I must, I said, give the true key to my whole life; *I must show what I am* . . . I wish to be known as *a living man* . . . I will draw out, as far as may be, the history of my mind . . .
>
> I have . . . few contemporary memoranda, I fear, *of the feelings or motives under which from time to time I acted* . . .
>
> I mean to be simply personal and historical: I am not expounding Catholic doctrine, I am doing no more than explaining myself, and my opinions and actions . . . It is not pleasant to reveal to high and low, young and old, *what has gone on within me from my early years.* It is not pleasant to be giving to every shallow or flippant disputant the advantage over me of knowing *my most private thoughts,* I might even say the intercourse between myself and my Maker.[6]

It should be noticed, in the first place, that Newman's focus is on himself. It is not on the Oxford Movement, it is not on doctrine or controversy, not on his family or his friends. He means "to be simply personal"; he is "doing no more than explaining" himself. In the next place, this personal focus is to be on his inner life. Outward events, except where closely connected with the history of his mind, are to be omitted. His subject is "what has gone on within me"; it is "my most private thoughts." Finally, and most important, the focus is to be on the whole sensibility. A history of the mind might have been a history of the intellect, of the evolution of ideas conceived ab-

6. *Apologia,* pp. 99–101. The italics are mine except for "mean."

stractly. That is not Newman's plan, as his phrasing makes evident. To describe the mind means for him to describe a "living intelligence." It means to show "what I am" and not merely "what I thought"; it means to set down "the feelings or motives under which from time to time I acted." Thus, in order to destroy Kingsley's caricature, Newman had to present a "living man," head and heart, reasons and emotions.

Given the intention, we are not surprised by the two elements of technique which Newman mentions in the same passage. "Letters from friends with some copies or drafts of my answers to them," together with other contemporary memoranda, would help enormously to recover opinions and motives forgotten or distorted by time and would be valuable insurance against errors, which could be very damaging under the circumstances.[7] Second, the use of small and personal details, apparently irrelevant, would expose the deeper sources of character and motive. "I may be accused of laying stress on little things, of being beside the mark, of going into impertinent or ridiculous details, . . . but this is a case above all others, in which I am bound to follow my own lights and to speak out my own heart." [8]

Certainly one would suppose that the Kingsley controversy had not only suggested the idea of the *Apologia* but had determined its nature and method as well. Yet this would be wrong. The truth is that there already lay in Newman's mind a series of long-standing, though dormant and unrelated, thoughts and attitudes which were capable potentially of combining for action, let the right stimulus occur: theories of rhetoric, conceptions of man and the psychology of faith, ideas about the art of style

7. *Idem,* p. 100.
8. *Idem,* p. 101; and cf. p. 105.

and the nature and methods of biography, including his own. The controversy determined nothing. It took a particular shape and that shape acted like a magnet. All the prerequisites were ready. When a lucky accident suggested autobiography, by still greater luck Newman was ready—marvelously equipped to write one of the great studies in human personality.

II THEORIES OF PSYCHOLOGY[9]

CONSIDER the primary notion of Newman's defending himself not with logic but with autobiography. He had always believed that logical demonstration was an ineffective weapon of persuasion, especially for a popular audience. "Logic makes but a sorry rhetoric with the multitude," he had said in 1841; "first shoot round corners, and you may not despair of converting by a syllogism." [10] And how can men be converted if "deductions have no power of persuasion"?

The heart is commonly reached, not through the reason, but through the imagination, by means of direct impressions, by the testimony of facts and events, by history, by description. Persons influence us, voices melt us, looks subdue us, deeds inflame us.[11]

9. I am indebted in this section to Lewis E. Gates, *Selections from the Prose Writings of John Henry Cardinal Newman* (1895), whose remarks on pp. xvi–xxiii I have adapted and developed. Gates's brief discussion and the original review by Samuel Wilberforce, *The Quarterly Review,* CXVI (1864), 528–573, seem to me the best, indeed almost the only illuminating, criticisms of the *Apologia.* Wilberforce's review is partly reprinted in *Famous Reviews,* R. B. Johnson, ed. (1914), pp. 288–305. Also worth consulting for occasional remarks are the original reviews by R. W. Church, *The Guardian,* June 22, 1864, reprinted in his *Occasional Papers* (1897, 2 vols.), II, 379–397, and by R. H. Hutton, *The Spectator,* XXXVII (1864), 654–656, 680–683. J. J. Reilly's chapters on "The *Apologia"* and "Newman as a Man of Letters" in his *Newman as a Man of Letters* (1925) are thin and superficial. The best general study of Newman's theory and practice of art, though lacking in critical perception, is by Tardivel (see p. 14, n. 21). Professor C. F. Harrold writes me that there is a section entitled "The *Apologia:* Its Method and Art" in his forthcoming book on Newman.

10. From "The Tamworth Reading Room" (1841), letter 6, in *Discussions and Arguments* (1882 ed.), p. 294.

11. *Idem,* p. 293.

It is not surprising that in 1864 Newman discarded logic for the rhetoric of autobiography and decided not to expound Catholic doctrine but "to be simply personal and historical, . . . simply to state facts." As Gates pointed out, the work is "persuasive because of its concreteness, its dramatic vividness, the modulations of the speaker's voice, the sincerity and dignity of his look and bearing." [12]

Such a biography could not be a history of ideas. It would have to cover the whole sensibility. This indeed followed independently from Newman's lifelong assumption that "man is *not* a reasoning animal; he is a seeing, feeling, contemplating, acting animal." [13] Though one might suppose, thinking first of his reputation for logical acuteness, that he was referring here only to "the multitude" and not to himself, that would be wrong. He said of his own progress to Rome that "it was not logic that carried me on"; and he added, "It is the concrete being that reasons . . . The whole man moves; paper logic is but the record of it." [14] This remark, significantly enough, is in the *Apologia*, for without that basic assumption Newman's biography would have been, like John Stuart Mill's, the life of an intellect and not, as it is, the life of a whole man.

The assumption dates from the *University Sermons.* There Newman first explored his theory that belief or faith was reached by a spontaneous instinctive process which logic could but analyze and chart, and that only roughly. The following description of the mind's activity, written in 1840, may well seem in retrospect a prophecy of what we find in the *Apologia:*

12. Gates, *Selections from Newman,* p. xxii.
13. *Discussions and Arguments,* p. 294.
14. *Apologia,* p. 264.

Theories of Psychology

The mind ranges to and fro, and spreads out, and advances forward with a quickness which has become a proverb, and a subtlety and versatility which baffle investigation. It passes on from point to point, gaining one by some indication; another on a probability; then availing itself of an association; then falling back on some received law; next seizing on testimony; then committing itself to some popular impression, or some inward instinct, or some obscure memory; and thus it makes progress not unlike a clamberer on a steep cliff, who, by quick eye, prompt hand, and firm foot, ascends how he knows not himself, by personal endowments and by practice, rather than by rule.[15]

That is the concrete being in the act of reasoning. For this *is* a process of reasoning, only reasoning, as Newman goes on to insist, "not by rule, but by an inward faculty" (here named "implicit reason," later the "illative sense"); it is "not an art," not logic or "explicit reason," but "a living spontaneous energy within us." [16] For Newman, then, any history of the mind and its changing beliefs would have to be the story—to return to his own words in the preface to the *Apologia*, whose background is now apparent—of "that living intelligence, by which I write, and argue, and act." It could not be a series of ideas developed in logical relationships.

He drew this conclusion himself, and in a significant connection. The problem of analyzing the spontaneous and inward process just described (the problem, it will be noted, of the autobiographer) was at best difficult; strictly speaking, impossible.

15. From "Explicit and Implicit Reason" (1840), in *Sermons, Chiefly on the Theory of Religious Belief, Preached before the University of Oxford* (1843), p. 252. Hereafter this book is referred to as *University Sermons*.
16. *Idem*, p. 253.

No analysis is subtle and delicate enough to represent adequately the state of mind under which we believe, or the subjects of belief, as they are presented to our thoughts. The end proposed is that of delineating, or, as it were, painting what the mind sees and feels; now let us consider what it is to pourtray duly in form and colour things material, and we shall surely understand the difficulty, or rather the impossibility, of representing the outline and character, the hues and shades in which any intellectual view really exists in the mind, or of giving it that substance and that exactness in detail in which consists its likeness to the original . . .

Is it not hopeless, then, to expect that the most diligent and anxious investigation can end in more than in giving some very rude description of the living mind, and its feelings, thoughts, and reasonings? [17]

Over twenty years later Newman set out to record not only his opinions, and by what "intelligible processes of thought" he came by them, but also "the feelings or motives" under which he acted.[18] And naturally enough, because his object was the same, he was still as acutely aware of the difficulty. "Who can know himself," he asked in the *Apologia*, "and the multitude of subtle influences which act upon him?" [19] Yet the very recognition of the difficulty was only possible to one who saw the problem clearly. His psychology told him that for autobiography even a "rude description of the *living* mind" was more central, because more faithful to experience, than any formal outline of logical developments. It also told him that even this rude description necessitated delving into the small and remote and often irrational forces which shape one's actions and trying to recover those exact details which in

17. *Idem,* pp. 263–264, from the same sermon.
18. *Apologia,* pp. 131 n., 100.
19. *Idem,* p. 191.

1864—and we now understand why—he was determined to use, even though they looked "beside the mark."

From the same premises another deduction would seem to follow. Since the individual, finding it hard enough to penetrate into his own motives, can scarcely hope to grasp those of others, and, since the reasoning process is, as Newman believed, so completely personal,[20] he might well prefer autobiography to biography, and for the latter insist on the closest possible approach to the former.

20. *An Essay in Aid of a Grammar of Assent* (1881 ed.), pp. 316, 317, 362, 364, 368. Hereafter this book is referred to as *Grammar of Assent*.

III THEORIES OF BIOGRAPHY AND
OF STYLE

NEWMAN's ideas on biography were not merely implicit in his conceptions of psychology. They had already been formulated. In the introduction to the "Last Years of St. Chrysostom" (1859–60) he had criticized "mere biographies" because their truth did not extend beyond exterior facts and events. "What I want to trace and study," he had said, "is the real, hidden but human, life, or the *interior*." [21] He wanted to see the underlying motives. These appeared, it was true, in the usual saint's life but they were supplied by the biographer out of his own head. "On the other hand, when a Saint is himself the speaker, he interprets his own action . . . His words are the index of his hidden life, as far as that life can be known to man, for 'out of the abundance of the heart the mouth speaketh.' " [22] And by good luck the ancient saints had left behind them "just that kind of literature which more than any other represents the abundance of the heart, which more than any other approaches to conversation; I mean correspondence." [23] The interconnection of these ideas is manifest in the important definition at which Newman finally arrives:

Perhaps I shall be asked what I mean by [a] "Life." I mean a narrative which impresses the reader with the idea of moral unity, identity, growth, continuity, personality. When a Saint converses with me, I am conscious of the presence of one ac-

21. *Historical Sketches* (1881 ed., 3 vols.), II, 219. Cf. Fernande Tardivel, *La Personnalité Littéraire de Newman* (1937), pp. 231–238, on Newman and biography.
22. *Historical Sketches*, pp. 220–221.
23. *Idem*, p. 221.

tive principle of thought, one individual character flowing on and into the various matters which he discusses, and the different transactions in which he mixes. It is what no memorials can reach.[24]

The imagination grasping the inner personality and embodying it so far as possible in a man's own words and thoughts and therefore through letters because they approximate conversation—that was Newman's theory; and plainly it was followed five years later in the *Apologia*.[25]

The theory, of course, was not new or original. There was Boswell before him. There was apparently a suggestion of Hurrell Froude's, and the example of both Froude and Stanley. In a letter of 1866 Newman said:

My own notion of writing a life is the notion of Hurrell Froude,—viz. to do it by letters, and to bring in as little letterpress of one's own as possible. Froude has so done his "Becket." It is far more real, and therefore interesting, than any other way. Stanley has so done in his "Arnold." [26]

As early as 1837 he had himself adopted this notion when he edited Froude's *Remains* and included a large number

24. *Idem*, p. 227.
25. Cf. the summary written in a letter of May, 1863, in *Letters and Correspondence of John Henry Newman*, Anne Mozley, ed. (1891, 2 vols.), I, 1: "It has ever been a hobby of mine, though perhaps it is a truism, not a hobby, that the true life of a man is in his letters . . . Not only for the interest of a biography, but for arriving at the inside of things, the publication of letters is the true method. Biographers varnish, they assign motives, they conjecture feelings, they interpret Lord Burleigh's nods; but contemporary letters are facts." Newman's conscious adoption of this theory for the *Apologia*, less than a year later, is emphasized by the list (*Apologia*, pp. 519–520) of "letters and papers of the author used in the course of this work." It is not, however, complete. The collection of Newman's letters edited by Anne Mozley is hereafter referred to as *Letters*.
26. Ward, *Life*, II, 314.

of letters "to show his mind, his unaffectedness, playful-
ness, brilliancy, which nothing else would show." [27] Such a
method exposes biography to the danger of excessive and
irrelevant detail, and Newman saw that selection was necessary. But he also saw that many a detail that looked
irrelevant carried an indirect reflection of character and
personality. He says in the preface to the *Remains:*

It may perhaps be thought, of the correspondence in particular, that it is eked out with unimportant details, according to
the usual mistake of partial friends. The compilers, however,
can most truly affirm, that they have had the risk of such
an error continually before their eyes, and have not, to the
best of their judgment, inserted any thing, which did not tell,
indirectly perhaps but really, towards filling up that outline
of his mind and character, which seemed requisite to complete the idea of him as a witness to Catholic views. [28]

Nearly thirty years later, in his own life, so full of letters,
we have noticed the same insistence upon "little things"
and on what may seem "impertinent or ridiculous details."

Though without expecting to use them himself, Newman had always taken special care of his letters. As early
as 1830 he wrote out to date "all that correspondence
which I mean to be a document to my heirs." [29] Then in
the years immediately preceding the *Apologia* he was
collecting and arranging his letters for a literary exec-

27. *Letters,* II, 237.

28. *Remains of the Late Reverend Richard Hurrell Froude* (1838–39,
4 vols.), I, xxi–xxii. Cf. *Letters,* I, 7. Still earlier, in 1828, apropos of a
possible memoir of his sister, he thought (*Letters,* I, 181) that the more
minute the circumstances recorded, the better.

29. *Letters,* I, 232. Almost certainly this is the body of letters, over
twenty in number, which passed between Newman, Dornford, Froude,
and Hawkins, dealing with the tutorial controversy. It is known that he
collected these letters in the summer of 1830. See Henry Tristram, "Two
Suppressed Passages from Newman's 'Autobiographical Memoir,'" *Revue Anglo-Américaine,* XI (1933–34), 482.

utor.[30] When he begged Copeland, his old Littlemore curate, whom he had met by chance the previous summer, to visit him in 1863 at the Oratory, he wrote, "You must come and look at my Letters. I only wish they were all in order." [31] And a little later, "You would be delighted to see Froude's letters to me" [32]—those letters which Newman once described as "of great value to me as a sort of journal from early boyhood nearly to the time of our separation [in 1836]." [33] And when, the next year, he decided to write his own life, he at once appealed to his old friends for further supplies. Especially for the years on his "death-bed," when perplexity and dismay left him less observant of himself and therefore less able, later on, to rely on memory, letters were almost indispensable.[34] That is why he wrote to Church particularly for "letters of mine" between 1841 and 1845 "to throw light on my state of mind"; [35] and why letters are used more often in that chapter than elsewhere.

In addition to correspondence, Newman also had at hand various fragments of autobiography. Setting aside the ambiguous case of *Loss and Gain*, there were the recollections he recorded in 1820 and 1823 of the "thoughts and feelings on religious subjects" which he had had in childhood and youth. Two of them reappeared on the opening pages of the *Apologia*.[36] A later page, on his

30. Ward, *Life*, II, 315–316. Later (*Letters*, I, 5, under date of 1884) he was to praise Anne Mozley's *Letters of J. B. Mozley* as answering his idea of a biography "because you have let him speak for himself"; and he commissioned the editor to do the same for his own life to 1845.

31. Ward, *Life*, I, 598.

32. *Ibid.*

33. *Letters*, II, 214.

34. *Apologia*, pp. 191, 245, show that Newman recognized these facts himself.

35. Ward, *Life*, II, 20.

36. *Apologia*, pp. 105–106.

Italian journey, was taken out of the description of "My
Illness in Sicily," which he wrote and rewrote at various
times between 1834 and 1840.[37] All in all, Newman was
not quite so unprepared with materials as he let it appear.[38]
Nor was he unprepared—and this was far more important,
considering how little time he had to plan the book or to
write it—with theories of biography, implicit in his *University Sermons* and explicit in "St. Chrysostom."

Already, too, he had articulated a theory of style so
consonant with his theory of biography as to argue their
mutual dependence. Saints' letters he had recommended
because they approached conversation. The same point
was made earlier about Froude's: "His letters approach to
conversation, to show his delicate mode of implying, not
expressing, sacred thoughts." [39] This virtue of letters,
Newman thought, should be the basis of all prose. His
ideal was a style that would be natural without being too
casual or abrupt, the ideal suggested by his directions on
how to write, sent to J. B. Mozley in 1838:

In what you write do not be too essayish: i.e. do not begin,
"Of all the virtues which adorn the human breast!" . . . be
somewhat conversational, and take a jump into your subject.
But on the other hand avoid abruptness, or pertness. Be *easy*
and take the mean—and now you have full directions how to
write.[40]

In Newman's mind is the same ideal described by Coleridge
when he advocated a natural style that should be "neither
bookish, nor vulgar, neither redolent of the lamp, nor of the

37. The "page" is *Apologia*, p. 135; the original accounts are in *Letters,*
I, 413-430.
38. Cf. *Apologia*, p. 100.
39. *Letters*, II, 237.
40. *Idem*, II, 256.

kennel"; in short, the style of "a gentleman . . . in dignified conversation." [41] Coleridge meant, of course, a gentleman trained at the Universities; and in Newman's case we may refer specifically to the Oriel common room, where conversation was a fine art. At any rate, that is Hopkins' account of the matter and it seems very likely. "Newman," he wrote to Patmore, "does not follow the common tradition —of writing. His tradition is that of cultured, the most highly educated, conversation; it is the flower of the best Oxford life." [42]

His tradition, no doubt, but adopted to serve deeper purposes than maintaining the tradition. The ultimate value of this style to Newman was its functional rôle in revealing the inner movement of mind, for at the center of his theory lay the conviction that style was personal and organic. The following sentences sum up the thesis of his lecture on "Literature" in 1858:

While the many use language as they find it, the man of genius uses it indeed, but subjects it withal to his own purposes, and moulds it according to his own peculiarities. The throng and succession of ideas, thoughts, feelings, imaginations, aspirations, which pass within him . . . *the very pulsation and throbbing of his intellect, does he image forth,* to all does he give utterance, in a corresponding language, which is as multiform as this inward mental action itself and analogous to it, *the faithful expression of his intense personality, attending on his own inward world of thought as its very shadow.*[43]

In short, the theories of biography and of style start from the same ambition, to image forth the inner life; and in

41. S. T. Coleridge, *Biographia Literaria,* J. Shawcross, ed. (1907, 2 vols.), I, 13–14; II, 23.

42. *Further Letters of Gerard Manley Hopkins,* C. C. Abbott, ed. (1938), p. 232.

43. In *The Idea of a University* (1901 ed.), p. 276. The italics are mine. Cf. *idem,* pp. 279–280, 285, 291–292.

both cases this is best achieved, Newman feels, through the medium of living speech, whether preserved in letters or now set down for the first time. The *Apologia* combined both methods in its faithful record of "his own inward world of thought."

IV POWERS OF MEMORY AND
INTROSPECTION [44]

F OR such an undertaking Newman himself was remark-
ably equipped. His memory of specific events, exterior and interior, was sharp and vivid. He was by nature
an introvert, and his theories of both conscience and belief
developed habits of introspection which made him un-
commonly aware of himself, though less successful in the
analysis of motive than is generally assumed.

On his own admission Newman had little power of re-
calling books or doctrines or arguments, but "in some
things," he added, "I have a good memory." [45] These things
were always concrete and personal. In 1861 he revisited
the house at Ham where he had lived as a child. "I have
never seen the house," he said, "since September 1807. I
know more about it than any house I have been in since,
and could pass an examination in it. It has ever been in
my dreams." [46] The final phrase is significant. Newman
did not merely think about his past; he relived it with all
the vividness and excitement possible in a dream. This can
be seen in the letter on revisiting Alton or in what he
called the "strange, dreamy reminiscences" of his Sicilian
illness, where the imagination revived the experience with
great fullness and precision of detail. [47]

His imagination also fastened on inner emotions more

44. The topics of this section have also been treated from another
angle by Tardivel, *La Personnalité Littéraire de Newman,* pp. 125–131,
on memory; *idem,* pp. 239–262 on psychological observation.
45. Ward, *Life,* II, 332.
46. *Letters,* I, 17, n.
47. *Idem,* II, 63–65; and *idem,* I, 413–430, for the illness; *idem,* I, 424,
for the quoted phrase.

than on outer facts and circumstances. Years later, in the *Grammar of Assent*, he decided that "the memory of countenances and of places in times past may fade away from the mind; but the vivid image of certain anxieties or deliverances never." [48] Anxieties and deliverances—that, of course, is the subject of the *Apologia*. No wonder the book owes so large a debt to Newman's hold on the inner qualities of old experience.

Why was his memory so alive? Partly, no doubt, because of his sensitive, introspective temper, but also because of an excessive absorption in the history of his own life. Much of his past hardly needed to be recalled; it was, so to speak, part of the present, like a surrounding atmosphere. The house at Ham is *ever* in his dreams. He is *haunted continually* by the faces of old friends.[49] Over and over again he writes the account of his illness in Sicily.[50] When we ask why this preoccupation with his past, two reasons come to mind, though of course there are many more. One is Newman's general belief in "Special Providences," and his particular belief that "a series of Providences" had been shaping his own life.[51] It is significant in this respect that the Sicilian experience, on which he dwelt so often, seemed to him then and later to be a divinely ordained penance and purification before undertaking the mission

48. *Grammar of Assent*, p. 25; and cf. p. 24, which is quoted just below in n. 55.

49. Ward, *Life*, I, 591.

50. *Letters*, I, 413–430.

51. For the general belief, *Sermons Bearing on Subjects of the Day* (1869 ed.), pp. 350–353, from No. 23; *Apologia*, pp. 231, 255; *Grammar of Assent*, p. 402; and Joseph Rickaby, *Index to the Works of John Henry Cardinal Newman* (1914), under "Providence." For the personal application, *Apologia*, pp. 135, 187, 214, 215, 314; *Letters*, I, 73, and II, 460–461; and especially the letter to Keble of June 8, 1844, in *Correspondence of John Henry Newman with John Keble and Others, 1839–1845*, edited at the Birmingham Oratory (1917), pp. 313–318. This book is referred to hereafter as *Correspondence*.

of 1833.[52] The second is his deep and lasting attachment to Oxford: to the friends that meant so much to him, to the time of life when he was happiest, to the place where "I was truly at home." [53] When he faced the act of conversion, he saw that it meant "sacrifices irreparable, not only from my age, when people hate changing, but from my especial love of old associations and the pleasures of memory." [54] In 1863 he wrote to Keble that even after twenty-five or thirty years the parishes of Hursley and Bisley (Keble's parishes where they had met so often) remained "photographed on my mind." And it was in the same letter that he said, "None *but* He, *can* make up for the loss of those old familiar faces which haunt me continually." [55] After 1845, and especially in the "Sad Days" of 1859-64 immediately preceding the *Apologia*, he clung desperately to his early hopes and friendships and affections. And this in turn, together with the immediate stimulus from rereading old letters, quickened his memory of precisely that Oxford life he was so soon and unexpectedly to be called on to describe. In these years, as Ward noted, "He would talk of its smallest details, which stood before his mind's eye with wonderful vividness." [56] He could hardly have been better prepared.

It is true that Newman often speaks of how difficult, if

52. *Apologia,* pp. 134–136; *Letters,* I, 412–414, 416, 418; *Correspondence,* p. 315.

53. *Apologia,* p. 174, is the best single entry. For his intense attachment to his friends, see the next sentences here in the text, and below on pp. 81–82, 111.

54. *Idem,* p. 320.

55. Ward, *Life,* I, 590, 591. Cf. *Grammar of Assent,* p. 24: "I see those who once were there and are no more; past scenes, and the very expression of the features, and the tones of the voices, of those who took part in them, in a time of trial or difficulty."

56. Ward, *Life,* I, 600, for this last quotation; chap. xix, called "Sad Days (1859–1864)," pp. 568–614, for the general state of mind described.

not impossible, it is to recapture the past,[57] but such remarks only testify, one might say, to his high standard of imaginative memory. In the midst of the Sicilian description he stops to remark, "I cannot quite tell whether or not I am colouring this, so let me say once for all that any descriptions of my feelings should be attended all through with 'I believe,' for I have half-recollections—glimpses which vanish when I look right at them." [58] Such a warning, far from weakening our confidence, assures us of a sensibility struggling to revive the furthest shades of experience; and for autobiography that is ten times more valuable than a mind which simply remembers the mere facts, however accurately.

Newman's delicate hold on the past was ultimately the result of what he himself described as his "vivid self-consciousness." [59] This had been fostered by a childhood imagination which could dissolve the material world until only the boy himself remained, in the company of angels; and presently by a religious conversion which, by making him rest in the thought of "two and two only supreme and luminously self-evident beings, myself and my Creator," further isolated him from surrounding objects and confirmed his mistrust of material reality.[60] Years later, with his own boyhood in mind, he spoke of a child's "intimate vision of God" as being his deepest sense of truth:

He listens, indeed, with wonder and interest to fables or tales; he has a dim, shadowy sense of what he hears about persons

57. Besides the quotation that follows, cf. *Apologia*, pp. 191, 245, and *Letters*, II, 437.

58. *Letters*, I, 421; and cf. a similar remark in *idem*, I, 318. I. A. Richards, *Practical Criticism* (1930), p. 217, notes that a "feeling even more than an idea or an image tends to vanish as we turn our introspective attention upon it. We have to catch it by the tip of its tail as it decamps."

59. *Letters*, I, 104.

60. *Apologia*, pp. 105–106, 108.

and matters of this world; but he has that within him which actually vibrates, responds, and gives a deep meaning to the lessons of his first teachers about the will and the providence of God.[61]

With obvious qualifications, that might also be said of Newman the man. Samuel Wilberforce, who knew him at Oxford and whose brother was his intimate friend, thought that "his hold upon any truth external to and separate from himself, was . . . feeble when placed in comparison with his perception of what was passing within himself." [62]

Though no doubt partly the product of such a temperament, two of Newman's major ideas must have confirmed this centripetal focus, while at the same time they served to encourage the deliberate self-analysis which in some degree always accompanies strong introversion and which in Newman amounted to a deeply rooted habit. The first was the importance of conscience, not simply for moral life but for Christian faith. Already in one of his earliest sermons Newman had reproved those who have only "general and vague impressions" of themselves and "who neglect the duty of habitual self-examination," "for it is in proportion as we search our hearts and understand our own nature, that we understand what is meant by an Infinite Governor and Judge"; and since without this inner knowledge all Christian doctrines remain verbal and external, Newman felt that we could profitably read the creeds and the Bible only "when we have experienced what it is to read ourselves." [63]

The other idea that promoted introspection came from his theory of knowledge mentioned earlier. If religious or

---

61. *Grammar of Assent*, pp. 113, 115.
62. *The Quarterly Review*, CXVI (1864), 546.
63. *Parochial and Plain Sermons* (1898, 8 vols.), I, 41–43, from Sermon IV, "Secret Faults."

moral truth was not to be obtained by any logical process, but only by that spontaneous, subjective movement of the mind described above, then one's conclusions were entirely personal.[64] They could not be subjected to any common or external test. If one questioned the results, he could only study the problem more widely, wait for the passage of time, and repeat the process.[65] In this way the problem of belief—and it was, of course, *the* problem of his earlier life —drove Newman in upon himself as it would not have driven a man more confident of an objective logical methodology.

Furthermore, there were degrees of belief which the individual had to detect and assess. Probabilities had to be measured "on a graduated scale of assent." Some might be numerous enough to create certitude; others sufficient only for opinion; still others only for a conjecture or perhaps no more than a possibility.[66] Whatever we may think of this *qua* theory, there can be no question that it provided the potential autobiographer with an unusual discipline of introspective analysis. In such a passage as the following from the *Apologia* we can watch Newman peering into the dark recesses of consciousness, trying to distinguish the subtlest shades of feeling and intuition. He is speaking of his increasing doubts about Anglicanism in 1842:

When my dissatisfaction became greater, it was hard at first to determine the point of time, when it was too strong to suppress with propriety. Certitude of course is a point, but

64. See the references for n. 15 and n. 20 above.
65. *Grammar of Assent,* p. 342. Newman's "appeal to time" has never, I think, been studied. Some of the source passages are: *Apologia,* pp. 215, 264–265, 307; *Grammar of Assent,* pp. 168–169, 255–258, 342; *Correspondence,* p. 218; *Sermons on Subjects of the Day,* pp. 357–359; *Essays Critical and Historical* (1901 ed., 2 vols.), I, 283. This last work is hereafter referred to as *Essays.*
66. *Apologia,* pp. 122–123.

doubt is a progress; I was not near certitude yet. Certitude is a reflex action; it is to know that one knows. I believe I had not that, till close upon my reception into the Catholic Church. Again, a practical, effective doubt is a point too, but who can easily ascertain it for himself? Who can determine when it is, that the scales in the balance of opinion begin to turn, and what was a greater probability in behalf of a belief becomes a positive doubt against it? [67]

67. *Idem,* p. 307; and, for another example, *idem,* p. 225.

V TECHNIQUE OF ANALYSIS

For the analysis of his mind Newman had at hand a technique ready for use. He had worked it out years before and described it in the important sermon on "Explicit and Implicit Reason." It involves two operations:

to designate particular methods of thought, according to which the mind reasons, (that is, proceeds from truth to truth,) or to designate particular states of mind which influence its reasonings. Such methods are antecedent probability, analogy, parallel cases, testimony, and circumstantial evidences; and such states of mind are prejudice, deference to authority, party spirit, attachment to such and such principles, and the like.[68]

These sentences, written in 1840, read like "Directions for Writing the *Apologia*."

So far as his development is explained by rational procedures, the burden falls on probability, because Newman was certain that in religious inquiry, unlike the exact sciences where rigid demonstration was possible, we "arrive at certitude by accumulated probabilities." [69] That is why for nearly every decision in the *Apologia* he gives not one but a number of converging reasons, no one of which, by itself, is convincing. Shall he resign St. Mary's? He sends Keble half a dozen arguments for thinking so. And, when Keble answers that his resignation would injure the Catholic cause and begs him to stay, he finds not one but three reasons why he ought to remain.[70] On a larger scale the

68. *University Sermons,* pp. 253–254.
69. *Apologia,* pp. 291–292.
70. *Idem,* pp. 228–232. For other examples, see *idem,* pp. 191–192, 205–206, 314–315.

same method is used for his conversion, since that rested, as he says, upon a series of probabilities:[71] that the Church of England was probably not a part of the Holy Catholic Church (which in turn rested on the analogy or "parallel cases" of Anglo-Catholics and Monophysites, and later Anglo-Catholics and Semi-Arians); that though it might have the power of the sacraments, nevertheless he himself probably could not be saved as an Anglican; that the so-called Roman errors were probably legitimate developments of primitive doctrine, and so on.

Roughly speaking, all this probing of his mind takes two forms: either what I shall call the "back-and-back" movement, each reason calling up, in turn, a deeper reason; or the "back-and-forth" movement, where the mind shifts and wavers between two opposing possibilities, exploring the pros and cons as they start into consciousness. Both processes will be illustrated later in the section on style.

Such "methods of thought," however, are less important than "particular states of mind." That is because Newman recognized how much the mental predisposition affected the weight of the evidence. Given a particular prejudice, a man will accept some reasons of the flimsiest kind or, conversely, reject others of the greatest validity.[72] Hence the mental make-up is as functional as the arguments themselves in determining religious faith. Indeed, it is really more decisive because it is basic:

Faith is influenced by previous notices, prepossessions, and (in a good sense of the word) prejudices, . . . less by evidence, more by previously-entertained principles, views, and wishes.

A man *is* responsible for his faith, because he is responsible

71. *Idem*, p. 292.
72. For sample statements see *University Sermons*, pp. 176–185, 219–223.

[29]

for his likings and dislikings, his hopes and his opinions, on all of which his faith depends.[73]

From such convictions we might have predicted, and rightly, that far less space in the *Apologia* would be devoted to rational arguments than to states of mind; and that most of Newman's attention would be placed on the likings and dislikings, the antecedent views and presumptions which prepared him to respond as he did to the ideas he encountered. Or to put it more exactly, since his subject was the evolution of his beliefs, he would have to show successive states of mind both before and after each new doctrine was met and assimilated. And that is precisely what he did. But not constantly and not pointedly. One must read slowly, with close reference to the full context, which sometimes means the entire volume, in order to perceive the bearing of many a fact or attitude which looks isolated and irrelevant.

Indeed, sometimes one can only guess; and sometimes one is baffled. This is important. Taken together with Newman's persistent failure to "point" the influence of attitudes upon beliefs, it means that he himself was often far from certain, no doubt often unaware, of their exact bearing upon his thought or action. It means that their functional rôle in the analysis of implicit reasoning is frequently overlooked or unclear, and that ultimately they come to hold an independent and autonomous life. They become pictures of "what the mind sees and feels" from moment to moment, with only the most tenuous connections, if any at all, with previous or later conclusions.

It is not surprising that the technique of designating "particular states of mind" should have come to stand alone. On the negative side, Newman had little faith in analysis. Pascal himself was not more convinced that the

73. *Idem*, pp. 179–180, 184.

heart has its reasons which the reason cannot know. The most diligent effort, Newman thought, can yield at best but a "very rude description of the living mind." "How a man reasons is as much a mystery as how he remembers." Faith is really unable "to analyze its grounds, or to show the consistency of one of its judgments with another." The "real" reasons for belief or action are precisely those least likely to be conscious, while those we exhibit in argument are selected because they are commonly received and credited.[74] These are Newman's premises. They do not encourage an autobiographer to try too hard to explain how and why he came to believe what he did. Certainly Newman was more concerned with how he was feeling and thinking at a given time than with why he so felt and thought. Indeed, one sometimes thinks he was more eager to engage the reader's imagination to relive his own (that is, Newman's) experience than to offer the reader's intellect a rational study in psychology. More than once he confesses that he did not understand the cause or source of a reaction which he has vividly described.[75]

And just as his theory of belief suggests a negative caution against attempting any close analysis, as impossible to achieve with success, it also suggests a positive attraction for details which might have no clear bearing on his development but which could serve admirably to reveal personality. If the reasoning process was too extensive, too complex and intricate, ever to be analyzed completely, then inevitably the attempt must yield, in part, irrational materials; that is, things clear in themselves but without any rational place in the chain of reasoning. Out of a mass

74. All references are to *University Sermons,* in order of the quotations, pp. 264; 255; 302–303; 260, 267–269.

75. See *Apologia,* pp. 135, 161, 213, which are quoted below on pp. 41, 42, 45, respectively. This thesis is explored again in my final section (sec. XI), where its bearing on the ultimate value of the book is estimated.

of probabilities, associations, laws, facts, memories, instincts, all combining in a final conclusion, only a few could be clearly seen in their causal position.[76] Others could be detected, though where or how they fitted would remain obscure. Yet certainly they must have been influential. They were part of the process. They ought to be included. In this way, states of mind, whose sole purpose in theory was to expose the deeper sources of motivation, in practice came frequently to be their own excuse for being, or, to speak more exactly, came to explain little but to reveal much.

Newman's preference for description over explanation has other sources than his theory of belief. From the start he had something of the romantic passion for experience however irrational, and this was given a religious sanction by his desire to save the "mysteries" of dogma. Both his letters and the *Apologia* contain details of action and feeling without significance or relation but included simply because he remembered them intensely and valued them as experience. The artist, in his conception, was not the neoclassical scholar or the modern intellectual but the romantic genius transcribing "the pulsation and throbbing of his intellect," or expressing his "intense personality." [77] Also, like so many of the romantics, Newman was fascinated by those undefined areas of existence which lie just out of reach, hovering elusively in the twilight of consciousness. "I wish it were possible," he says in 1828, "for words to put down those indefinite, vague, and withal subtle feelings which quite pierce the soul and make it sick." [78] And it was

76. *University Sermons*, pp. 252–253, partly quoted above, p. 11.
77. *The Idea of a University*, p. 276. And cf. *idem*, p. 329, where he complains that what our writers lack is "individuality . . . which is the greatest charm of an author."
78. *Letters*, I, 184.

possible—for Newman. At the age of eighteen he was already wrestling with the definition of emotion:

Sunday evening bells pealing. The pleasure of hearing them. It leads the mind to a longing after something, I know not what. It does not bring past years to remembrance; it does not bring anything. What does it do? We have a kind of longing after something dear to us, and well known to us—very soothing. Such is my feeling at this minute as I hear them.[79]

Analysis is baffled, but the emotion is sharply recorded, the personality is revealed.

This concern with what lies beyond "fact and reason," so characteristic of romanticism, demands what Keats called "*Negative Capability*, that is, when a man is capable of being in uncertainties, mysteries, doubts, without any irritable reaching after fact and reason." [80] The advantage? For Keats, the sense of beauty was preserved; for Newman, the sense of divinity. Protesting against a rationalism which would limit revelation to what is clear and logical and so rob religion of all that is awesome and mysterious, Newman pled for the value "of half views and partial knowledge, of guesses, surmises, hopes and fears, of truths faintly apprehended and not understood." [81] Thus, even apart from his theory of belief, it would seem predestined that the history of his own religious experience would include feelings and intuitions that eluded rational explanation.

79. *Idem,* I, 52.
80. Letter to George and Thomas Keats, December 28, 1817, in *The Letters of John Keats,* M. B. Forman, ed. (1931, 2 vols.), I, 77. Cf. Lamb's contrast of himself with a typical Scotchman in "Imperfect Sympathies," *The Essays of Elia.*
81. From "Tracts for the Times," No. 73 (1836), in *Essays,* I, 34. Cf. F. L. Cross, *John Henry Newman* (1933), pp. 82–84.

From the preceding discussion we should be prepared to find that Newman's analytic method in action gives more attention to "states of mind" than to "methods of thought"; [82] that sometimes "states of mind," when the context is noted, have a definite bearing (whether intentional or not we cannot tell and we do not care) on Newman's reasoning; and that sometimes they stand alone, without apparent explanation or significance beyond themselves.

82. It is true, however, that the arguments are more conspicuous because rhetorically they are given major emphasis. This is discussed and accounted for below, pp. 100–102. But underneath, so to speak, the states of mind are more pervasive and fundamental.

PART TWO

METHOD AND STYLE

VI THE ANALYTIC METHOD IN ACTION

THE opening pages of the *Apologia* are designed to lay down the earliest tendencies or prejudices of Newman's mind, its original shape, so to speak, which was ready to receive or to reject various ideas it was to encounter—say, Evangelicalism and Utilitarianism, for examples of both possibilities. In rapid succession he mentions his mystical imagination that finds this world an illusion, the crossing of himself on going into the dark, his drawing the figure of a cross in a schoolbook, his reaction to the skepticism of Hume and Voltaire—so revealing of both his personal immunity to and his keen understanding of doubt—"how dreadful, but how plausible!" [1] A little later he does not overlook the effect of Newton's argument for the Pope being Antichrist: "The thought," he adds in words which reflect the unified character of his mind, "remained upon me as a sort of false conscience." [2] At the same time "another deep imagination" took possession of him, that it was the will of God he should lead a single life. And this in turn, he is careful to point out with his eye fixed on the resulting state of mind, "strengthened my feeling of separation from the visible world." [3]

When we come to the powerful influences of Froude and Keble, how little is said of their intellectual arguments against either Evangelical or Liberal Protestantism. Newman centers on his own states of mind, in the one case after,

1. *Apologia,* pp. 105–107.
2. *Idem,* p. 110.
3. *Idem,* pp. 110–111.

in the other before, his association. Take the significant conclusion to the paragraphs on Froude:

> It is difficult to enumerate the precise additions to my theological creed which I derived from a friend to whom I owe so much. He made me look with admiration towards the Church of Rome, and in the same degree to dislike the Reformation. He fixed deep in me the idea of devotion to the Blessed Virgin, and he led me gradually to believe in the Real Presence.[4]

In anyone else the first sentence would surely have introduced a list of dogmas. In Newman it leads to "the hues and shades in which any intellectual view really exists in the mind." [5] He does not say that Froude "made me think" so-and-so for such-and-such reasons, but "made me look" with likings and dislikings, the very factors on which for Newman, we remember, faith depends.[6] And the *idea* of devotion to the Virgin was *fixed deep* in his sensibility. The Roman "state of mind" is seen taking shape.

The case of Keble illustrates the complementary method, the setting down of the preëxisting attitude without which we could hardly understand Newman's ready acceptance of his theology. Before we ever hear a word of Keble's thought, we are first told of the day when the great man was pointed out in High Street by Bowden, who cried out, " 'There's Keble!' and with what awe did I look at him!" [7] And then we hear of their first meeting on the occasion of the Oriel election when Newman was receiving the congratulations of the Fellows. "I bore it," he says, "till Keble took my hand, and then felt so abashed and unworthy of the honour done me, that I seemed desirous of quite sinking into the ground." It is easy to pass

4. *Idem,* pp. 126–127.
5. *University Sermons,* p. 263, quoted above on p. 12.
6. See above, pp. 29–30.
7. *Apologia,* p. 119. This is also the reference for the next anecdote.

over these details merely as "vivid memories," but in point of fact they are there to reveal a state of mind prepared to receive Keble's teaching with the readiest sympathy. Nor is that merely a deduction from Newman's theory of belief. It is supported by the placing of both incidents out of their chronological order, in the opening paragraph on Keble as the primary author of the Oxford Movement.

This illustration has a wider bearing. It also reveals both Newman's general deference to authority, which it should be recalled is one of his sample "states of mind," and his particular subjection to personal influences. Again and again he brings out the warmth of his affections for the men whose ideas he might not otherwise have found attractive, for Thomas Scott and Edward Hawkins, for example, or Whately and Pusey.[8] Nothing could show this better than the concluding sentences on the Monophysites. By the logic of analogy Newman saw himself as a Monophysite forging arguments against the authority of the Apostolic Church. But this logic would scarcely have carried conviction had it not been translated by Newman into personal terms:

What was the use of continuing the controversy, or defending my position, if, after all, I was forging arguments . . . against the much-enduring Athanasius and the majestic Leo? Be my soul with the Saints! and shall I lift up my hand against them? . . . anathema to a whole tribe of Cranmers, Ridleys, Latimers, and Jewels! perish the names of Bramhall, Ussher, Taylor, Stillingfleet, and Barrow from the face of the earth, ere I should do aught but fall at their feet in love and in worship, whose image was continually before my eyes, and whose musical words were ever in my ears and on my tongue![9]

8. *Idem,* pp. 108, 111, 114, 161.
9. *Idem,* pp. 211–212.

The Art of Newman's Apologia

We remember the earlier dictum: "Persons influence us, voices melt us, looks subdue us." [10] And I would argue that the *Apologia* is, in fact, a record of such influences far more than a record of advancing logic (is not argument swallowed up in an access of personal devotion to Athanasius and Leo?) and that the acceptance of the logic, here and elsewhere, is only credible, as Newman's theory would predict, in the light of his emotional bias.

The exploration of previous and subsequent states of mind can be studied in larger perspective if we concentrate on the year 1833. Newman returned home in early July, heard Keble's Assize Sermon on the next Sunday, and at once threw himself into the new movement with every ounce of thought and energy, writing most of the early tracts, calling on clergymen all over the country, corresponding with others, doing a series of letters in the *Record* on church reform, and so on. Such positive and public action, so uncongenial to his natural temper,[11] is explicable only in the light of the frame of mind with which he returned to England; and that had been clearly sketched in the closing pages of the previous chapter.

The paragraphs on Newman's Italian journey are among the finest in the book.[12] His distaste for foreign life and travel, coupled with his distress at the success of the Liberal cause (the bill for the suppression of the Irish Sees was in progress), created a state of intense longing for home and action. His "fierce thoughts against the Liberals" are illustrated by two telling details:

10. *Discussions and Arguments*, p. 293. For Newman's recognition of how strongly people influenced him, see *Apologia*, p. 159, and *Letters*, I, 416; II, 156. For his doctrine of personality see *Apologia*, pp. 132, 135, 142–144; *Letters*, I, 463–468; and W. R. Castle, Jr., "Newman and Coleridge," *Sewanee Review*, XVII (1909), 139–152.

11. Newman says so himself in *Apologia*, p. 145.

12. *Idem*, pp. 133–136, from which all the following quotations are taken.

A French vessel was at Algiers; I would not even look at the tricolour. On my return, though forced to stop a day at Paris, I kept indoors the whole time, and all that I saw of that beautiful city, was what I saw from the Diligence.

Froude chooses the motto for *Lyra Apostolica,* begun at Rome: " 'You shall know the difference, now that I am back again.' " Especially when alone, the thought comes upon Newman "that deliverance is wrought, not by the many but by the few, not by bodies but by persons." He keeps repeating words dear to him since schooldays, "Exoriare aliquis." Cardinal Wiseman, as their interview closes, hopes he and Froude will make a second visit to Rome, but Newman replies gravely, " 'We have a work to do in England.' " He goes down to Sicily, the sense of mission growing stronger, and falls ill. Then follow some sentences which show at a glance the priority of "awareness" over "analysis" in Newman's temper and writing:

My servant thought that I was dying, and begged for my last directions. I gave them, as he wished; but I said, "I shall not die." I repeated, "I shall not die, for I have not sinned against light, I have not sinned against light." I never have been able to make out at all what I meant.

I got to Castro-Giovanni, and was laid up there for nearly three weeks. Towards the end of May I set off for Palermo, taking three days for the journey. Before starting from my inn in the morning of May 26th or 27th, I sat down on my bed, and began to sob bitterly. My servant, who had acted as my nurse, asked what ailed me. I could only answer him, "I have a work to do in England."

Two irrational incidents which any other pre-Freudian biographer would certainly have excluded and which even now, years after the event, Newman will not attempt to explain. And yet how absolutely authentic—precisely the right degree of incoherence that would occur under the delirium of fever. And we can feel, if we cannot see clearly, the connection of the sobbing and the two remarks with the whole fixation of the English mission. Then, in the last paragraph, the rush to get back to England with its sickening delays and frustrations before he finally reaches home on a Tuesday. "The following Sunday, July 14th, Mr. Keble preached the Assize Sermon in the University Pulpit." Is it any wonder that Newman threw himself into the Oxford Movement with exuberant and joyous energy? Or that he rejected the arguments for Palmer's Association to defend the Church and insisted on supporting the "antagonist principle of personality," deliverance to be wrought not by bodies but by persons? [13]

But he is not content with explaining his new temper as merely one of energetic and supreme self-confidence. He goes on to show how, under the circumstances, his behavior took on a mixture of fierceness and of sport, described and illustrated in detail, and how he developed a "lounging, free-and-easy way of carrying things on." [14] He concludes with a revealing remark. "All this," he says, referring to his tolerant acceptance of coworkers who did not share many of his views, "may seem inconsistent with what I have said of my fierceness. *I am not bound to account for it.*" [15]

At the next crisis of his life, in 1839, Newman takes even greater pains to expose the prior state of mind without which neither the logical nor emotional impact of the event can be understood. "In the Spring of 1839," he begins, "my position in the Anglican Church was at its height. I had supreme confidence in my controversial *status*, and I had a great and still growing success, in recommending it to others." [16] These statements are followed by an exten-

13. Cf. *idem,* pp. 142–144 with 135.
14. *Idem,* pp. 146–150, 158–161.
15. *Idem,* p. 161. The italics are mine.
16. *Idem,* p. 192.

sive digest of an article in the *British Critic* because this
"will best describe my state of mind at the early part of
1839." [17] Then comes a further section, complementing the
previous description of his general confidence with an exposition of where he stood on the controversy between Rome
and the Anglican Church. Though acknowledging that
this must be dry discussion, Newman defends its insertion
as being "as necessary for my narrative, as plans of build-
ings and homesteads are often found to be in the proceedings of our law courts." [18] Necessary, that is, because in
both cases we must know the lie of the land in order to
understand what took place. We need to know Newman's
supreme confidence to appreciate the terrific force of a misgiving utterly unexpected and quite unprepared for. And
we need to know that Newman took his stand on Antiquity
(the Anglican Church maintains the primitive doctrine
without the later Roman Catholic errors) against the Roman stand on Catholicity (there is but one Holy, Catholic
Church and the English Church is in schism) to appreciate
the logical impact of his sudden discovery that Antiquity
itself upheld the principle of Catholicity.

When the blow comes, we see it strike the whole man, for
Newman is concerned not with the argument as an argument—that came later—but simply with its impact upon
him. Take a passage like this:

The principles and proceedings of the Church now, were those
of the Church then; the principles and proceedings of heretics
then, were those of Protestants now. I found it so,—almost
fearfully; there was an awful similitude, more awful, because
so silent and unimpassioned, between the dead records of the
past and the feverish chronicle of the present. The shadow of
the fifth century was on the sixteenth. It was like a spirit

17. *Idem*, p. 193.
18. *Idem*, pp. 201-202.

rising from the troubled waters of the old world, with the shape and lineaments of the new.[19]

The same fullness of reaction is caught again in the succeeding account of Wiseman's article on the parallel between the Anglicans and the Donatists, that both were in schism. The friend who showed Newman the article pointed to the crucial quotation from Augustine:

"Securus judicat orbis terrarum." He repeated these words again and again, and, when he was gone, they kept ringing in my ears. "Securus judicat orbis terrarum;" they were words which went beyond the occasion of the Donatists: they applied to that of the Monophysites. They gave a cogency to the Article, which had escaped me at first. They decided ecclesiastical questions on a simpler rule than that of Antiquity; nay, St. Augustine was one of the prime oracles of Antiquity; here then Antiquity was deciding against itself. . . . The deliberate judgment, in which the whole Church at length rests and acquiesces, is an infallible prescription and a final sentence against such portions of it as protest and secede. Who can account for the impressions which are made on him? For a mere sentence, the words of St. Augustine, struck me with a power which I never had felt from any words before. To take a familiar instance, they were like the "Turn again Whittington" of the chime; or, to take a more serious one, they were like the "Tolle, lege,—Tolle, lege," of the child, which converted St. Augustine himself. "Securus judicat orbis terrarum!" By those great words of the ancient Father, interpreting and summing up the long and varied course of ecclesiastical history, the theory of the *Via Media* was absolutely pulverized.[20]

As before, we do not have a separate treatment of the "idea" and the "response." Both are woven together exactly as

19. *Idem*, p. 211.
20. *Idem*, pp. 212–213.

they were for Newman, united and fused in that haunting phrase that rang in his ears. And why so intense a reaction? The argument, which is highly debatable, does not explain it. Only the preceding state of mind, so carefully sketched, together with still earlier states of mind, like that produced by Froude or seen in his passionate devotion to Leo and Athanasius,[21] can make it credible, though scarcely more. In its review of the *Apologia*, *The Saturday Review* mentioned three reasons why Newman went to Rome, one of them being "a certain passage in St. Augustine which operated on a harassed, susceptible, and fluctuating mind like a charm, or a Divine Voice, or a special interposition of some kind or other." [22] Precisely. There is no adequate explanation. And Newman sees this himself: *he cannot*, he says, *account for the impression.* Yet the impression itself is sharply conveyed. No question we see before us a living, breathing human being, however short we are of understanding him.[23]

21. See, respectively, the quotations above on pp. 38, 39–40.
22. *The Saturday Review*, XVII (1864), p. 786.
23. For a similar analysis of Part VI, which might have been placed here, see below, pp. 109–111.

VII STYLE AND THE DRAMATIC
RE-CREATION OF THE PAST

R EVELATION that is sharp and full requires the most sensitive control of language. Diction, imagery, rhythm,
syntactical structure must work together to express the
whole movement of the mind, the very curve, so to speak,
of the "living intelligence." Is this true for Newman? That
is the critical question; and it can be answered only after
close analysis. What makes the usual approach to Newman's style so sterile (and this may be said of prose criticism in general) is the tendency to treat style as a separate
entity. At its worst this produces the long catalogue of his
various styles which scholars like to isolate and describe:
his Ciceronian style, his Gibbonian style, his Attic and his
Hebraic styles, his regal, elegiac, or academic styles, and so
on. Or, if that approach is discarded, we get a list of certain devices common to all his writing: his three types of
phrasing (simple, "curled," and cumulative), his homely
diction, his sententious wit, his poetic rhythms, and the
like, each with examples pulled out of their contexts. This
approach is better but still far from illuminating. It is only
when we study such devices in action, when we see them func-
tioning in a given sentence, that we become, through this
knowledge, more sensitive to meaning. Then only is our
reading deepened. Prose criticism needs to ask a new question: not "What *are* the characteristics of this man's
style?" but "What do they *do?* How do they function?" or,
specifically in the case of the *Apologia*, we want to know
how closely the technique is the medium of felt experience.
Then, if we conclude that Newman's style is a great style,

it will not be because it is beautiful or ingenious or homely, or because of any other quality supposed inherent in various techniques, but because it is organic.

Newman was quite clear about this himself. It is the thesis of his lecture on "Literature" in 1858. Critics who think of "fine writing" as something to be added to the matter "speak as if *one* man could do the thought, and *another* the style." But "matter and expression are parts of one: style is a thinking out into language." [24] His application of this principle to psychological fidelity, partly quoted earlier, must now be set down fully and with italics to bring out a further implication:

While the many use language as they find it, the man of genius uses it indeed, but subjects it withal to his own purposes, and moulds it according to his own peculiarities . . . *The very pulsation and throbbing of his intellect,* does he image forth, to all does he give utterance, in a corresponding language, which is as multiform as *this inward mental action* itself and analogous to it, the faithful expression of his intense personality, attending on his own inward world of thought as its very shadow. . . . His thought and feeling are personal, and so his language is personal.

An organic style, of course, may take various forms. From all that we know of Newman—from his vivid memory, from his doctrine of personality (explicit in this quotation) and his intense self-consciousness, from his belief in special providences with its tendency to make life seem a series of dramatic events, from his theory of biography and his way of seeing the mind never as static but always in action (note the italicized phrases)—from all these factors we could be certain that for his purpose in the *Apologia* an organic

24. *The Idea of a University,* pp. 277, 276. The latter is also the reference for the quotation that follows.

style would be a dramatic style. That is to say, it would embody his own immediate reëxperiencing of the past. It would project "the very pulsation and throbbing of his intellect."

Newman's re-creation of psychological life can be studied in four principal techniques. First, in his syntax, where the clausal arrangement, length, and connectives are conditioned not by any esthetic feeling for beauty but simply by the desire to give, in external outline, the inner pattern and movement of his thinking. Second, there is the skillful use of metaphor to define emotion or to project the fusion of thought and feeling. Since Newman does not merely remember the past but relives it with a unified sensibility, metaphor enables him to express the full complex of idea and emotion. Third, by the use of a conversational idiom, in diction and rhythm, he can translate the clash of ideas back into their original human context. It enables him to avoid setting down the old arguments in expository form and, instead, to return them, so to speak, to their living existence when they were first debated in passionate speech, whether with actual opponents or with himself, talking out loud. In a passage from his journals where Newman laments his lack of original ideas and his tendency to adopt those of others, especially Keble's, he consoles himself with the thought that at least he has "a rhetorical or histrionic power to represent them." [25] Finally, the *Apologia* is dramatic in its narrative settings, which recapture the suspense, the circumstantial detail, the climax, and "wild surmise" of past events, whether external or internal.

Part V, from 1839 to 1841, opens with a paragraph that reveals Newman's state of mind as he was writing and reveals it through most of his normal modes of expression. It

25. *Letters,* I, 416.

is so valuable a text for our present study that I quote most of the passage:

And now that I am about to trace, as far as I can, the course of that great revolution of mind, which led me to leave my own home, to which I was bound by so many strong and tender ties, I feel overcome with the difficulty of satisfying myself in my account of it, and have recoiled from doing so, till the near approach of the day, on which these lines must be given to the world, forces me to set about the task. For who can know himself, and the multitude of subtle influences which act upon him? and who can recollect, at the distance of twenty-five years, all that he once knew about his thoughts and his deeds, and that, during a portion of his life, when even at the time his observation, whether of himself or of the external world, was less than before or after, by very reason of the perplexity and dismay which weighed upon him,—when, though it would be most unthankful to seem to imply that he had not all-sufficient light amid his darkness, yet a darkness it emphatically was? And who can suddenly gird himself to a new and anxious undertaking, which he might be able indeed to perform well, had he full and calm leisure allowed him to look through every thing that he has written, whether in published works or private letters? but, on the other hand, as to that calm contemplation of the past, in itself so desirable, who can afford to be leisurely and deliberate, while he practises on himself a cruel operation, the ripping up of old griefs, and the venturing again upon the "infandum dolorem" of years, in which the stars of this lower heaven were one by one going out? [26]

If we ask what this paragraph is about, we have to answer that it is about a problem, the problem of writing autobiography under the circumstances, but also it is about the man who is thinking and feeling the problem. The full sensibility is given dramatic expression.

26. *Apologia*, pp. 191–192.

The Art of Newman's Apologia

A. Syntax

THE rhetorical questions reveal the exact patterns of Newman's self-analysis mentioned earlier.[27] In the second sentence the mind is seen pushing "back-and-back," each time to a deeper obstacle still remaining even if the previous one were removed. The increasing length and complication of phrasing, from the first to the second to the third question, suggest the increasing complexity and difficulty of knowing himself.[28] Below we find a slightly different form to fit a difference in introspective movement, not so much "back-and-back" as "back-and-forth." The difficulty caused by the need for immediate performance would be obviated, he thinks, if only he had full calm and leisure to examine letters and works; "but, on the other hand" such calm contemplation, "*in itself so desirable*," would be impossible under such painful circumstances.

The placing of the phrase I have italicized is a warning against any quick definition of this second type of syntax as simple antithesis. What we see is not a mind in balanced suspense, facing two contrasting views, but rather a mind in the very act of shifting back and forth or of weaving in and out. The italicized phrase could easily have gone with the previous clause, after the word "leisure," for instance. Then we should have had a clear contrast. As it is, Newman's mind has gone on to the contrast, then slipped back to the value of contemplation, then quickly returned to its evils. Another example is necessary to see how faithfully Newman's syntax is made, in this way, to reflect the characteristic oscillation of his mind. He is speaking of his mixed feelings about the group of young Anglican Romanists who "cut

27. Above, p. 29.
28. For other examples of this "back-and-back" pattern, see *Apologia*, pp. 187 (ll. 9–13), 215 (ll. 8–16), 225 (ll. 14–25).

into the original Movement at an angle" about 1839 and formed a new party different from the earlier Tractarians:

> Though I neither was so fond (with a few exceptions) of the persons, nor of the methods of thought, which belonged to this new school, as of the old set, though I could not trust in their firmness of purpose, for, like a swarm of flies, they might come and go, and at length be divided and dissipated, yet I had an intense sympathy in their object and in the direction of their path, in spite of my old friends, in spite of my old life-long prejudices. In spite of my ingrained fears of Rome, and the decision of my reason and conscience against her usages, in spite of my affection for Oxford and Oriel, yet I had a secret longing love of Rome the author of English Christianity, and I had a true devotion to the Blessed Virgin.[29]

The structure here is so intricate and involved, the meaning so hard to follow at first reading, that one is tempted not to praise the style but to charge it with unnecessary awkwardness and obscurity. One thinks by contrast of how clearly a man like J. S. Mill would have said the same thing:

> On the one hand, I was not so fond of the persons, nor of the methods of thought, which belonged to this new school, as of the old set. As for the persons, I could not trust in their firmness of purpose, and I felt greater love for my old friends. As for the methods, I still retained my old life-long prejudices and my ingrained fears of Rome, and the decision of my reason and conscience was against her usages. On the other hand, I did have an intense sympathy in their object, and in the direction in which their path lay because I had a secret longing love of Rome, the author of English Christianity, as well as a true devotion to the Blessed Virgin.

No question, I think, that the neatly balanced structure I attribute to Mill gives the passage a clarity and ease that

29. *Idem,* pp. 260–261.

is lacking in Newman. And yet, in return for that sacrifice (and it is a deliberate sacrifice: he could, of course, write with perfect clarity of form when he chose), Newman's structure has caught and projected the very sense of wavering, of being pulled back and forth and forth and back, which he was undergoing. A diagram is the best way to show this oscillation. The left direction marks disapproval of the new group, the right, approval.

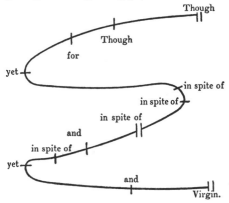

By contrast, the statement attributed to Mill would look like this:

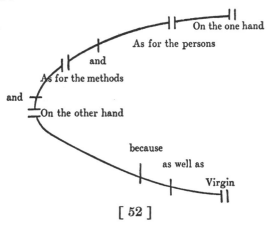

Style and the Re-creation of the Past

It is true that in neither form could Mill have written this sentence, and I do not mean because of what it says. I mean because it balances conflicting attitudes without coming to any resolution. Mill's mind was inclusive and synthetic: he always tried to bring ideas together, to mediate between old and new. Newman's mind was exclusive and separatist: he tried to reject one idea and take the other, with the result, as here, that he often got caught in the middle, uncertain which way to turn and for the moment looking alternately in both directions.[30] His style renders this dilemma superbly.[31]

B. Metaphor and Imagery

IN THE *University Sermons* Newman spoke of how difficult it was to delineate or, as it were, paint "what the mind sees and feels."[32] If we substitute "what the mind thinks," we grasp his meaning more exactly by noticing what we lose, and thereby realize again how faithful he was to the wholeness of experience. A moment later he amplifies this insight: one must try to represent "the outline and character, the hues and shades in which any intellectual view really exists in the mind." One must try to capture not the "thought" but the "tone of thought." To succeed in articulating such a complex of "idea" and "emotion," the all-but-indispensable instrument is metaphor. And Newman was a master of metaphor.

In the paragraph from which we started, the muscular tension is immediately felt as Newman "recoils" from his task of tracing a revolution which led him to leave his "own home," to which he was "bound by so many strong and ten-

---

30. *Idem,* p. 110 on the doctrine of Antichrist is an excellent illustration.
31. For other examples, see *idem,* pp. 147 (from l. 32) to 148 (l. 8), 155 (from l. 32) to 156 (l. 13), 252 (ll. 18–24). Notice the reference to syntax in the quotation from Yeats which I apply to Newman, below, p. 61.
32. *University Sermons,* p. 263, quoted above, p. 12.

der ties," until the dead-line "forces" him to set about it. And, below, he must suddenly "gird himself" for the undertaking; that is to say, must rouse and prepare and nerve himself against his desire, all those connotations fused together. Again, a little above, the third difficulty is not ascribed simply to a state of perplexity and dismay but to "perplexity and dismay which weighed upon him"; and this is followed by the visual weight, so to speak, of the emphatic darkness, pierced only by a ray of light. Still further, the analysis of the past is a "cruel operation," a "ripping up of old griefs"; and then, with a fine transition from pain to the profound note of sorrow, it becomes "a venturing again upon the 'infandum dolorem' of years, in which the stars of this lower heaven were one by one going out." The use of "infandum dolorem," incidentally, is not in the least pedantic. The very sound, apart from the meaning, reverberates with sadness, and, moreover, the phrase is plainly intended to recall the opening of the *Æneid*, Book II, and thus sharpen and intensify the expression of Newman's own situation by the analogy with *Æneas*, meeting a similar demand to recount painful events of the past, and with a similar reluctance:

> Infandum, regina, iubes renovare dolorem.
> Troianas ut opes et lamentabile regnum
> eruerint Danai, quaeque ipse miserrima vidi
> et quorum pars magna fui. . . .
>
> .   .   .   .
>
> Sed si tantus amor casus cognoscere nostros
> et breviter Troiae supremum audire laborem,
> quamquam animus meminisse horret luctuque refugit,
> incipiam.[33]

33. Translated by Charles J. Billson, *The Æneid of Virgil* (1923), p. 30, as follows:
           "Unutterable, O Queen, the pain thy words

Style and the Re-creation of the Past

Finally, the force of Newman's images is increased and pointed, as is often the case, by their integration. The darkness of perplexity becomes, below, the darkness of this lower heaven as the stars were going out.

So also in the paragraphs on the Monophysites and the Donatists we can now see how the fusion of idea and feeling, already insisted upon,[34] is partly conveyed by metaphor, and how the metaphors are reinforced by patterns of repetition. After his first reading Newman says he thought "the shadow of the fifth century was on the sixteenth." And then he continues, with a nice modulation from one type of shadow to another, "it was like a spirit rising from the troubled waters of the old world, with the shape and lineaments of the new." [35] Two pages later, after the Donatist article, his summary not only picks up the same imagery but develops on an alternating pattern of statement and reaction in which the same images are used, respectively, as dead and live metaphors:

I became excited at the view thus opened upon me . . . After a while, I got calm, and at length the vivid impression upon my imagination faded away . . . I had to determine its logi-

> Bid me revive; how Troy's great realm of woe
> Fell to the Greek, what piteous scenes I saw
> And was great part of . . .
>   Yet if so strong thy wish
> To learn in brief our woes and Troy's last hour,
> Although my memory shudders and recoils,
> I will assay."

Newman's famous description of Virgilian sadness is in the *Grammar of Assent*, pp. 78–79. It may be noted, in passing, that the idea for the fine image of the stars going out one by one, which concludes the sentence that quotes "infandum dolorem," was almost certainly suggested by Virgil's lines in the same passage:
> . . . et iam nox umida caelo
> praecipitat suadentque cadentia sidera somnos.

34. Above, pp. 44–45.
35. *Apologia*, p. 211.

[55]

cal value, and its bearing upon my duty. Meanwhile, so far as this was certain,—I had seen the shadow of a hand upon the wall. It was clear that I had a good deal to learn on the question of the Churches, and that perhaps some new light was coming upon me. He who has seen a ghost, cannot be as if he had never seen it. The heavens had opened and closed again. The thought for the moment had been, "The Church of Rome will be found right after all;" and then it had vanished. My old convictions remained as before.[36]

Only close analysis, however rough and clumsy, can show how neatly Newman has here projected the shifting impact, now on his mind, now on his imagination. The view that first opens upon him is without metaphorical value; it is an "idea." But in the second sentence, also linked to the first by the transition from "excited" to "calm," the view becomes, so to speak, a real view, a vivid impression, an illumination that gradually faded away. The sensory connotation of light is now distinctly noticeable in both "vivid" and "faded." Then, after the shift back to abstraction (he had to determine its logical value), we return to Newman's imagination, and the view again becomes something seen, the shadow of a hand. In similar fashion the abstract statement about seeking fresh light on the question of the churches is followed by the concrete sight of a ghost and then by the view of the heavens opening and closing, where we almost catch the flash of actual light. (Those verbs, incidentally, are closely linked with the previous "opened" and "faded.") Finally, in the summary sentence, idea and image, which so far have been alternating, are brilliantly fused in "vanished," which at once carries the "view" as idea (I had that thought about Rome, then I forgot it; it vanished) ; and the "view" as concrete image (the impression, the shadow, the ghost, the glimpse of heaven, all gone,

36. *Idem,* pp. 213–214.

blotted out—vanished). Writing of this kind has the fullness and integration of great poetry. It is closer to the earlier seventeenth century than to the middle nineteenth.[37]

C. Diction and Rhythm

IF WE return once more to our starting paragraph, we can take it as characteristic of Newman's natural speech. Its style is slightly too formal for actual conversation (the rhetorical questions give a studied effect), but we catch the impression of a man who is writing down his *spoken* thoughts, who is composing, that is, dramatically.

This leads, for one thing, to the use of homely and sometimes racy idiom. Though Newman's use of this device has often been noted, its precise effect in the *Apologia* has not, because no allowance has been made for the different impressions a homely diction may convey in different contexts. Its effect is one thing in Herbert's *Country Parson;* in *Pilgrim's Progress* another; still another in the dramatic context of the *Apologia*, where it carries the suggestion of the human voice talking right out, either today in 1864 or with the suggestion that this was Newman's original spontaneous speech on the occasion described. In a sentence like "I was sore about the great Anglican divines, as if they had taken me in, and made me say strong things, which facts did not justify," [38] we catch the immediate sense of a man protesting against being tricked. To discard the phrasing for something more dignified, for "I was annoyed with the great Anglican divines, as if they had concealed the truth with sophistries," is, of course, to drain the life from Newman's re-creation of the past. Still more sharply,

37. For some other examples of Newman's use of metaphor and imagery, see *idem*, pp. 174 (ll. 22–31), 266–267 (the paragraph on life at Littlemore), 344 (ll. 6–9).
38. *Idem*, p. 219.

don't we hear his living protest in the following sentences on why he refused to withdraw Tract 90? "How could I acquiesce in a mere Protestant interpretation of the Articles? how could I range myself among the professors of a theology, of which it *put my teeth on edge*, even to hear the sound?" [39]

There, of course, the colloquial expression is only one element in the dramatic effect. The passage as a whole depends on another form of spoken thought, the use of fiery rebuttal rather than logical exposition when Newman is on the defensive, answering his opponents. For a better example we may take his reply to those who insisted that, since the Articles were framed against popery, they could not possibly support Roman Catholic doctrine. Here is the answer as he *might* have written it:

The Popery which England hated in the sixteenth century was not Roman Catholic doctrine; it was the supremacy of the Pope. That was the great question in the days of Henry and Elizabeth. So far as doctrine was concerned, they were both rather pro-Catholic and anti-Protestant. Henry believed in purgatory and attacked justification by faith alone. Elizabeth had no conscientious scruples against the mass, and she never liked the marriage of the clergy. Therefore, when the articles were framed, hostility to Popery did not mean hostility to Roman doctrine but to Roman jurisdiction.

That, as I say, is how Newman *might* have defended himself, years later, from an old charge. But, instead of any such expository argument, this is what we find in the *Apologia:*

39. *Idem,* p. 187. The italics are mine. For other examples of racy speech, see *idem,* pp. 140 (l. 22), 141 (l. 8), 143 (l. 24), 154 (l. 14), 160 (l. 12), 193 (l. 13), 225 (l. 12), 246 (l. 17), 261 (l. 16), 264 (l. 24), 276 (l. 27), 283 (l. 2).

Not any religious doctrine at all, but a political principle, was the primary English idea of "Popery" at the date of the Reformation. And what was that political principle, and how could it best be kept out of England? What was the great question in the days of Henry and Elizabeth? The *Supremacy;* —now, was I saying one single word in favour of the Supremacy of the Holy See, in favour of the foreign jurisdiction? No; I did not believe in it myself. Did Henry VIII. religiously hold Justification by faith only? did he disbelieve Purgatory? Was Elizabeth zealous for the marriage of the Clergy? or had she a conscience against the Mass? The Supremacy of the Pope was the essence of the "Popery" . . . at the time of the composition of the Articles.[40]

Are we to call this merely a rhetorical device to enliven abstract material? Is it not rather the imaginative re-creation of his own reaction at the time—the excited and irritated answer he made to himself, talking out loud as anyone does at such a moment? (Did I ever say that? No! I didn't believe it myself! Was Henry a Protestant? or Elizabeth?)

On another occasion, worth quoting for its variation of the same method, Newman himself has confirmed the impression we get of creative memory. The subject is the impertinent infringement of the newspapers upon his privacy at Littlemore. He begins by dramatizing the attack: "Reports of all kinds were circulated about me. 'Imprimis, why did I go up to Littlemore at all? For no good purpose certainly; I dared not tell why.' "[41] This is first met by some caustic irony. "It was hard that I should be obliged to say to the Editors of newspapers that I went up there to say my prayers . . . I was considered insidious, sly,

40. *Idem*, p. 179.

41. *Idem*, p. 266; and the quotations that follow extend to p. 267. All italics are mine.

dishonest, if I would not open my heart to the tender mercies of the world." Then, a return to indirect discourse. "But they persisted: 'What was I doing at Littlemore?'" Whereupon, dropping the expository defence, Newman breaks out into direct and dramatic denunciation:

> Doing there? have I not retreated from you? have I not given up my position and my place? am I alone, of Englishmen, not to have the privilege to go where I will, no questions asked? am I alone to be followed about by jealous prying eyes, who note down whether I go in at a back door or at the front, and who the men are who happen to call on me in the afternoon? Cowards! if I advanced one step, you would run away; . . . Why will you not let me die in peace? Wounded brutes creep into some hole to die in, and no one grudges it them. Let me alone, I shall not trouble you long.

And then suddenly comes a remark of the first critical value:

> This was the keen feeling which pierced me, and, I think, *these are the very words that I used to myself.*

Whether they are the very words or not makes no difference. Literal accuracy is immaterial because autobiography is an art. All that Newman's words have to do is to convey the essential quality of his past experience; and to do that Newman himself must relive the experience imaginatively. That is what his statement proves. He has again felt the same keen feeling, talked back again as he did in 1842, no doubt pacing his study, muttering half aloud. As Hopkins once said, "What Cardinal Newman does is to think aloud, to think with pen to paper." [42] But the creative process which I think lies behind many a

42. *Further Letters,* p. 232.

page of the *Apologia* and explains so much of its success is best described by Yeats's account of his own method. When something stirred his imagination he began, he says, talking to himself, dramatizing himself, sometimes speaking and moving as if he were still young. These soliloquies caught his interest "by their accurate description of some emotional circumstance, more than by any aesthetic value." His one object in writing was "to find for them some natural speech, rhythm and syntax." [43]

D. Dramatic Structure

Finally, Newman dramatizes his life in another way. Its great events—the return to England in 1833, the summer reading of 1839, the reception of Tract 90, his ultimate conversion—these were Newman's climactic moments, intensely felt and intensely remembered. In retrospect, therefore, he sees them dramatically, that is, as scenes in a play, each with its elements of irony, suspense, circumstantial detail, marked climax, and, over all, the presiding sense of Providence, very like fate or "the gods."

The return to England has been commented upon earlier. Here we need only notice that, with Newman frantic to get home, the tension is built up by a series of delays: the long illness in Sicily, the three weeks waiting for a vessel at Palermo, another week becalmed in the Straits of Bonifacio; at length Marseilles and the road for England, only to be laid up several days at Lyons exhausted from travel; then "at last I got off again, and did not stop night or day, (excepting the compulsory delay at Paris,) till I reached England." The suspense thus created (it is nicely maintained by the last parenthesis) and the sense of emotions dammed up to explosion point (the detail about "writing verses the whole time of my passage" increases the feeling

43. *The Autobiography of William Butler Yeats* (1938), p. 452.

of nervous tension) prepare together for the climax, which in turn gains added edge from its position at the end of the chapter:

At last I got off again, and did not stop night or day, (excepting the compulsory delay at Paris,) till I reached England, and my mother's house. My brother had arrived from Persia only a few hours before. This was on the Tuesday. The following Sunday, July 14th, Mr. Keble preached the Assize Sermon in the University Pulpit. It was published under the title öf "National Apostasy." I have ever considered and kept the day, as the start of the religious movement of 1833.[44]

The circumstantial detail is very effective: his brother's arrival a few hours before . . . that was on Tuesday . . . on Sunday, Keble's sermon. Finally, in the full context one is aware—it is not explicit, but none the less felt, and felt dramatically—of the Hand of God: the purgatorial illness and then the return at exactly the crucial moment to begin a divine mission.

This event, however, is not quite typical. It was the only exciting narrative Newman had to relate and he cautions the reader at the start of the next chapter not to expect anything else in similar vein: "In spite of the foregoing pages, I have no romantic story to tell." [45] Nevertheless, if on a more subdued level, the inner crises of his life are developed with the same dramatic movement. Part V, from 1839 to 1841, opens with the ominous announcement that he is about to trace "that great revolution of mind, which led me to leave my own home," but we do not reach the revolution for twenty pages—another form of delay with similar effect of suspense. In the meanwhile he will describe

44. *Apologia*, pp. 135–136, for the whole passage. The previous discussion is above, pp. 40–42.
45. *Idem*, p. 139.

his state of mind, he says, by digesting an article in the *British Critic* for April, 1839. And then follow some remarks that throw a flash of light on the creative process I am illustrating:

I have looked over it now, for the first time since it was published; and have been struck by it for this reason:—it contains the last words which I ever spoke as an Anglican to Anglicans. It may now be read as my parting address and valediction, made to my friends. I little knew it at the time.[46]

We can see Newman here in the very act, so to speak, of dramatizing his past. In the light of events, what irony —this confident defence of Anglicanism his last words! He little knew it at the time! Eight pages later the digest closes on the same note of suspense and irony:

And thus I left the matter. But, while I was thus speaking of the future of the Movement, I was in truth winding up my accounts with it, little dreaming that it was so to be;—while I was still, in some way or other, feeling about for an available *Via Media*, I was soon to receive a shock which was to cast out of my imagination all middle courses and compromises for ever.[47]

At this point, with his reader keyed to expectation, Newman at last starts to move forward. "As I have said," he goes on, "this Article appeared in the April number of the British Critic; in the July number, I cannot tell why, there is no Article of mine; before the number for October, the event had happened to which I have alluded." And then, as we wait, impatient, for the answers—what event? when? why?—Newman quietly continues, "But before I proceed to describe what happened to me in the summer of

46. *Idem,* p. 193.
47. *Idem,* p. 201, which is also the reference for the quotations just below in my text.

1839, I must detain the reader for a while, . . ." the "while" being for another eight pages, explaining where he then stood on the Roman controversy. No wonder that when we finally reach the great event the suspense is high. And even then Newman does not come at once to his climax. He sets the stage. The little matter-of-fact details are like the lull before a storm:

The Long Vacation of 1839 began early. There had been a great many visitors to Oxford from Easter to Commemoration; and Dr. Pusey and myself had attracted attention, more, I think, than in any former year. I had put away from me the controversy with Rome for more than two years. In my Parochial Sermons the subject had never been introduced: there had been nothing for two years, either in my Tracts or in the British Critic, of a polemical character. I was returning, for the Vacation, to the course of reading which I had many years before chosen as especially my own. I have no reason to suppose that the thoughts of Rome came across my mind at all.[48]

At long last, against this total background, comes the climax—first, the fact of doubt and, second, the doubt itself:

About the middle of June I began to study and master the history of the Monophysites. I was absorbed in the doctrinal question. This was from about June 13th to August 30th. It was during this course of reading that for the first time a doubt came upon me of the tenableness of Anglicanism. I recollect on the 30th of July mentioning to a friend, whom I had accidentally met, how remarkable the history was; but by the end of August I was seriously alarmed.

I have described in a former work, how the history affected me. My stronghold was Antiquity; now here, in the middle of the fifth century, I found, as it seemed to me, Christendom of the sixteenth and the nineteenth centuries reflected. I saw my face in that mirror, and I was a Monophysite. The Church

48. *Idem*, p. 210.

of the *Via Media* was in the position of the Oriental communion, Rome was, where she now is; and the Protestants were the Eutychians.[49]

In the first sentences the circumstantial detail of dates, in the new paragraph the striking metaphor of the mirror and the slow heavy beats ("Rome was, where she now is") are superb. The single flaw is the irrelevant and distracting reference to a previous account.

Finally, in another mode, Newman's last departure from Oxford is also seen dramatically. Nothing could show this better than a comparison with his diary account of the same event:

Feb. 22. . . . Fly came for me and my luggage at four o'clock to take me to Johnson's, where I dined with Lewis, Buckle, Copeland, and Bowles, who came from Hendred. Church and Pattison came in the evening. Called on Ogle. Pusey came up to Johnson's late at night to see me.

Feb. 23. Went off by 8½ o'clock with Bowles for Maryvale via Leamington. Got there before 5 o'clock.[50]

These, so to speak, are the bare bones. In the *Apologia* they have not only become flesh, but flesh quivering under dramatic tension. The moment was, indeed, charged with pathos. Newman was breaking the deepest ties of friendship; he was leaving forever the place which had been his world and his home for thirty years. That is what we are made to realize almost painfully:

I slept on Sunday night at my dear friend's, Mr. Johnson's, at the Observatory. Various friends came to see the last of me; Mr. Copeland, Mr. Church, Mr. Buckle, Mr. Pattison, and Mr. Lewis. Dr. Pusey too came up to take leave of me; and I called on Dr. Ogle, one of my very oldest friends, for he was

49. *Idem*, pp. 210-211.
50. Ward, *Life*, I, 116–117.

my private Tutor, when I was an Undergraduate. In him I took leave of my first College, Trinity, which was so dear to me, and which held on its foundation so many who have been kind to me both when I was a boy, and all through my Oxford life. Trinity had never been unkind to me. There used to be much snapdragon growing on the walls opposite my freshman's rooms there, and I had for years taken it as the emblem of my own perpetual residence even unto death in my University.

On the morning of the 23rd I left the Observatory. I have never seen Oxford since, excepting its spires, as they are seen from the railway.[51]

What gives that passage its special force and quality is the sense of hard-won restraint. The passionate outbreak is held in. The language is kept simple. The atmosphere is strikingly still. And the use of commonplace detail has the same dramatic effect as Lear's "pray you, undo this button" or Beatrice's remark as she is led off to die, "Here, Mother, tie My girdle for me, and bind up this hair In any simple knot." This technique can only succeed, of course, if we are already aware of the pain that lies just beneath the surface. Then the pathos is doubled by such a heroic act of simplicity and self-control in the very face of suffering that might well excuse a violent or angry outburst, and suffering which already in itself has won our pity. From the first sight of Keble on through the whole book Newman's profound attachment to Oxford has been built up; and now, as he comes to leave, he drops two remarks, quoted from letters of the time, which bring this background immediately to our minds. "How much I am giving up in so many ways!" he says a few pages earlier, "and to me sacrifices irreparable, not only from my age, when people hate changing, but from my especial love of old associations

51. *Apologia*, p. 327.

and the pleasures of memory." [52] And then, just before the final passage, another letter is quoted: "You may think how lonely I am. 'Obliviscere populum tuum et domum patris tui,' has been in my ears for the last twelve hours." [53] It is because we know his grief that the final passage carries dramatic pathos to the highest level.

52. *Idem,* pp. 319–320.
53. *Idem,* p. 327. The quotation, appropriately enough, is from the verses of Psalm 45 which extol the sacrifice of home and friends for the sake of the Lord.

VIII THE MOTIVE OF APOLOGY AND ITS INFLUENCE ON STYLE

NEWMAN's book can be looked at in two ways, and these have sometimes been spoken of as though they were incompatible. Is it an autobiography? Or is it an apology? Ward referred to some readers for whom the *Apologia* belongs "to the literature of self-revelation, not to apologetic." Gates thought people who regarded it as "frank autobiography" were quite wrong; it is "an enormously elaborate and ingenious piece of special pleading." For Harrold, however, "the *Apologia* is in no sense an 'apology'; it is a candid revelation of the inner and outer facts of Newman's experience." [54] But must we, or indeed should we, choose between these assumptions?

To Newman, surely, the book was both. He spoke of it as the history of his mind, the picture of "what I am," the record of his feelings and motives, and so on.[55] Years later, long after the controversy was over, he was ready to accept the *Apologia* as an adequate account of his life from 1833 to 1845.[56] Yet he also insisted that "my main purpose . . . is a defence of myself"; he begged the reader to remember that "I am but vindicating myself from the charge of dishonesty"; he appealed to the British public as if to a jury and predicted that he would vanquish "not my Accuser, but my judges." [57] Most conclusive of all is

54. Ward, *Life*, I, 3; Gates, *Selections from Newman*, p. xix; C. F. Harrold, ed., *A Newman Treasury* (1943), p. 363.
55. *Apologia*, pp. 99–101; cf. *idem*, pp. 131 n., 211.
56. *Letters*, I, 5.
57. *Apologia*, pp. 338, 131 (from the first edition only), 99, respectively. See also *idem*, p. 88, and the letter of 1875 where he says (Ward, *Life*, II, 46) that Kingsley gave him the wished-for opportunity "of vindicating my character and conduct in my 'Apologia.'"

the statement in the preface to the first edition, a year after the chapters had appeared separately as pamphlets. He would like, he says, to wipe out of the volume all traces of the originating circumstances, but this is not possible because the title of *Apologia* "is too exactly borne out by its matter and structure." [58] In the face of these remarks, we cannot disregard the influence of an apologetic motive.

And the probability is strengthened when we remember Newman's long study and use of rhetoric. In a well-known passage he described himself as a person without ideas or convictions of his own but with "rhetorical or histrionic power to represent" those he adopted from others.[59] Anne Mozley noted the subtle variation of his style, even in his letters, to harmonize with the known character of each correspondent; [60] and the same awareness of his audience appears everywhere in his published works. He shrewdly estimates the degree of resistance he must expect—and counteract—from the prejudices or preoccupations of his readers. He skillfully alters his means with every change in end.[61] How could we expect this not to be also true in the *Apologia*, of all places?

Yet such an admission need not impugn the claim of sharp and faithful revelation. In every work of history or biography there has to be selection and emphasis. Certain

58. *Apologia*, p. 483.
59. *Letters*, I, 416; cf. *idem*, II, 156.
60. *Idem*, I, 9.
61. Gates, *Selections from Newman*, pp. xiii–xvi, is an excellent short account of Newman's rhetorical training. With the *Apologia* specifically in mind, Gates remarks (p. xvi): "The shape which his discussion finally took,—the particular methods that he followed,—were the result of a deliberate adaptation of means to ends; they were the methods that *his trained rhetorical instinct and his insight into the truth he was handling* and into the temperaments and intelligences he was to address himself to dictated as most likely to persuade." The italics are mine; they bear on what follows just below in my text.

materials have to be chosen, certain traits of character have to be stressed. On what principle? In Gibbon, let us say, speaking broadly, to show the formation of the historian; in Mill, to show the growth of a mind toward synthesis in an age of clashing philosophies; in Newman, to defend himself. Apology is simply one of many, and absolutely necessary, disciplines for the biographical imagination. But, it will be said, one of the most dangerous. So it is, and we shall have to inquire if Newman's picture is too favorable. But men *have* defended themselves by stating the truth.[62] For the moment we simply ask how has Newman's desire to defend himself affected the artistic process?

Centrally, as I just said, by the selection of material. What I mean can be illustrated if we ask why Newman describes his state of mind at the start of the Movement in such detail. He suggests the answer himself when he points out that his behavior "had a mixture in it both of fierceness and of sport, . . . [which] gave offence to many." [63] Hence it was necessary partly to acknowledge the fault and partly to justify and palliate it by explaining his peculiar emotional bias at the time. He thus cites a series of examples which at once "apologize" and reveal. "I used irony in conversation," he says, "when matter-of-fact men would not see what I meant," which both illuminates the man and accounts for his being misjudged.[64] Everywhere, I suggest, though often less obviously, the primary object of defence has, so to speak, been at Newman's elbow, telling him what to select and when to analyze.

The same object lies behind certain techniques already attributed to the "pure" intention of self-revelation, which is but another proof that the motives worked together and

62. See the italicized remark in the preceding footnote.
63. *Apologia,* p. 146.
64. *Idem,* p. 147.

that the *Apologia* is not a combination of two things but an integrated whole. Letters and journals, quotations from books or articles, all serve both the defendant and the psychologist with first-hand contemporary evidence. "You might have letters of mine to throw light on my state of mind," he wrote to Church in April, 1864; and then added, "and this by means of contemporaneous authority." [65] The same dual object is served by his "speaking" style. It not only gives remembrance the impact of immediacy; it has all the winning effect of simplicity, sincerity, and intimacy.[65a] No rhetorical flourishes, no pontificating, no abstruse phrasing and technical jargon, but a living voice speaking out simply and directly to every reader. And this simplicity acts as a guarantee of sincerity, a quality of the utmost importance for his rebuttal of Kingsley's charge. Newman had remarked, in the lecture on "Literature," that, when a man sincerely gives forth "what he has within him," his style inevitably has "the charm of an incommunicable simplicity." [66] And many a reader must have agreed with the person who spoke of Newman's being so "absolutely himself in his power of writing" and added that this was "an example of his nature and his gift of what is called *simplicity*." [67] Nor should we overlook the flattering sense of intimacy which one picks up, however unconsciously, from the confidential tone, not to mention the reassuring kinship one feels with a great prelate who can speak of giving his opponents "tit for tat," of being "sore" at the Anglican divines who had "taken me in," or

65. Ward, *Life*, II, 20.
65a. Cf. Hopkins, *Further Letters*, p. 232, writing of Newman's style: "His tradition is that of cultured, the most highly educated, conversation. . . . Perhaps this gives it a charm of unaffected and personal sincerity which nothing else could."
66. *The Idea of a University*, p. 292.
67. *Letters*, I, 9.

of having "a lounging free-and-easy way of carrying things on." In these ways we see Newman's style exemplifying his dictum that "persons influence us, voices melt us." [68]

The impression of sincerity derived from the style merges into the more positive appreciation of Newman's candor. Every reader of an apology is suspicious, and in this case it seemed quite possible that John Bull would get not only a slick piece of special pleading, with all Newman's sins and errors whitewashed, but also a militant blast at the English Church, along with some nice Roman proselytizing. Newman was much too smart for any of that. It was all well and good, some years before, to smooth over certain difficulties in Catholic teaching for an Anglican audience of prospective converts. But now his audience was the British public and they were to judge not doctrine but a man, and a man accused of being sly, devious, and sophistical. The only possible reply was to show himself a man of remarkable candor, concerned only to state the facts and eager to see both sides of every question—in short, completely objective and impartial.

Time and again Newman disclaims any intention of preaching, or indeed even of defending his beliefs and actions beyond claiming that they were honestly reached. In the preface he announced:

I mean to be simply personal and historical: I am not expounding Catholic doctrine, I am doing no more than explaining myself, and my opinions and actions. I wish, as far as

68. For the source, see p. 9, n. 11. R. W. Church's note on "Cardinal Newman's Naturalness" (in *Occasional Papers,* II, 479–482), which relates these stylistic qualities to his personal manners, closes with the remark that Newman believed "he could win the sympathy of his countrymen, though not their agreement with him; and so, with characteristic naturalness and freshness, he wrote the *Apologia.*"

The Motive of Apology

I am able, simply to state facts, whether they are ultimately determined to be for me or against me.[69]

And this disclaimer is astutely repeated at two crucial moments: when he first doubts the truth of Anglicanism and when he is finally converted to Rome. "Now let it be simply understood," he reminds the reader in the first case, "that I am not writing controversially, but with the one object of relating things as they happened to me." And, in the second, "Let it be recollected that I am historically relating my state of mind . . . I am not speaking theologically, nor have I any intention of going into controversy, or of defending myself." [70] This repeated denial is reassuring.

Furthermore, the objective attitude seems confirmed by the impartial admission of errors and difficulties—in his personal conduct and thinking, in Roman Catholicism, in religious faith itself—along with impartial praise for the English Church. In such ways Newman skillfully makes himself appear calm, reasoned, fair-minded, only concerned with the bare facts, whether or not they help or hinder his cause—all of which, of course, was precisely the best possible defence.[71] This is not to admit distortion, or to deny it; the whole question is postponed until later.

69. *Apologia,* p. 101. Part VII is a partial exception, and only partial because even there the emphasis is nicely placed on "me" rather than on "you," that is, on why Newman holds this or that Catholic doctrine rather than on why his reader ought to hold it. In any case, the narrative ends with Part VI, as Newman points out (*idem,* p. 331).

70. Respectively, *idem,* pp. 211, 291–292.

71. The impression made upon R. W. Church, *Occasional Papers,* II, 382, is probably true for most readers. He could not recall another story of conversion "which is so generous to what he [Newman] feels to be strong and good in what he has nevertheless abandoned, so fearless about letting his whole case come out, so careless about putting himself in the right in detail; which is so calm, and kindly, and measured, with such a quiet effortless freedom from the stings of old conflicts."

A man may really be calm, reasoned, and fair-minded, and still have to use plenty of skill to convince his judges that that is in fact his character.

Consider Newman's frequent confession of faults and mistakes, sometimes by way of accepting the truth of old charges, at least substantially (he rarely omits some qualification), but sometimes thrown in apparently gratuitously with a wonderful air of both humility and confidence, as though he were at once repentant for his sins and yet quite certain they were too few and too small to damage his cause. Of Dr. Hawkins, for example, he is sure he has often provoked him, and that "in me such provocation was unbecoming." [72] At the opening of the Movement, he confesses, his behavior "had a mixture in it both of fierceness and of sport" which gave offence to many; "nor am I here defending it." [73] And then he sets down blunt examples of both. In this book, written to justify his successive changes of belief, he is candid enough to admit that

. . . persistence in a given belief is no sufficient test of its truth; but departure from it is at least a slur upon the man who has felt so certain about it. In proportion then as I had in 1832 a strong persuasion in beliefs which I have since given up, so far a sort of guilt attaches to me, not only for that vain confidence, but for my multiform conduct in consequence of it.[74]

Even more satisfactory is his facing up to the appalling desertion and denial of the Anglican *Via Media:*

I heard once from an eye-witness the account of a poor sailor whose legs were shattered by a ball, in the action off Algiers in 1816, and who was taken below for an operation. The sur-

72. *Apologia,* p. 111.
73. *Idem,* p. 146.
74. *Idem,* p. 150.

geon and the chaplain persuaded him to have a leg off; it was done and the tourniquet applied to the wound. Then, they broke it to him that he must have the other off too. The poor fellow said, "You should have told me that, gentlemen," and deliberately unscrewed the instrument and bled to death. Would not that be the case with many friends of my own? How could I ever hope to make them believe in a second theology, when I had cheated them in the first? with what face could I publish a new edition of a dogmatic creed, and ask them to receive it as gospel? Would it not be plain to them that no certainty was to be found anywhere? [75]

What makes this so effective is the form of expression. Are not those the very gibes which the suspicious reader would like to make? And here they are, and in an "apologia," and even in Newman's own mouth! He does not say, "I suppose the reader may wonder how I expected to make people believe in a second theology," but "how could *I* ever hope to make them believe . . . when *I* had cheated them." It was he himself, then, who first asked these embarrassing questions, fearlessly and honestly! And the word "cheated" is a masterpiece. "When I had misled them," or "misguided them," or "led them astray," or half-a-dozen other variations could hardly have been called euphemisms. But *cheated them*—how unnecessary and how wonderfully fair for Newman to state the case at its worst! Surely he must have some very ingenious excuse up his sleeve to take the sting out of that. And he has an excuse, a feeble excuse, which he saves by confessing its weakness—which in turn reflects credit on his fairness:

Well, in my defence I could but make a lame apology; however, it was the true one, viz. that I had not read the Fathers critically enough; that in such nice points, as those which

75. *Idem,* p. 297, which is also the reference for the next two passages quoted.

determine the angle of divergence between the two Churches, I had made considerable miscalculations.

This might well have closed the matter. But Newman hears another objection on the reader's lips and again asks the awkward question himself, and again, by doing so, produces the impression of concealing nothing. "And how came this about?" Then a fresh apology, equally feeble, and therefore again tempered with the same judicious minimizing of its force:

And how came this about? Why, the fact was, unpleasant as it was to avow, that I had leaned too much upon the assertions of Ussher, Jeremy Taylor, or Barrow, and had been deceived by them. Valeat quantum,—it was all that *could* be said.

Much the same impression, so unexpected and so very effective in an apology, appears in his treatment of Roman Catholicism. Newman does not omit his former attacks; indeed, he reprints some savage words against the political machinations of the clergy and their methods of proselytizing. He quotes his charge of 1840 that they were "attempting to gain converts among us by unreal representations of its doctrines, plausible statements, bold assertions, appeals to the weaknesses of human nature, to our fancies, our eccentricities, our fears, our frivolities, our false philosophies." [76] And so through a long paragraph which could well have been omitted and surely would have been, except that its very presence here, in 1864, does credit to the man who would not suppress it—and, still more, would not retract it, for though he laments having made such insinuations, he does not deny their truth. Even apart from Roman practices, which, of course, many good

76. *Idem,* p. 223.

Catholics condemn, Newman is honest enough to admit his difficulties. On devotions to the Virgin he remarks: "*I say frankly*, I do not fully enter into them now." [77] Later, in the fine chapter on Catholicism, he begins one paragraph, "Now I will go on *in fairness to say* what I think *is* the great trial to the Reason, when confronted with that august prerogative of the Catholic Church." [78] And his conversion? Is it a sublime moment when the veils were lifted and the Truth at last rushed into his soul? when he came finally, in weariness and ecstasy, to rest in the divine bosom of Mother Church? That is what we expect and may well be ready to write off as the conventional unction of a Roman convert. And what do we get?

I was not conscious to myself, on my conversion, of any difference of thought or of temper from what I had before. I was not conscious of firmer faith in the fundamental truths of revelation, or of more self-command; I had not more fervour; but it was like coming into port after a rough sea; and my happiness on that score remains to this day without interruption.[79]

Could anything be better? The apparent effort not to make a single false claim and not to boast of the least improvement in himself. Then the reserved and measured statement.

In the same way, to the same affect, Newman candidly admits the difficulties of faith itself. He makes no easy or superior assumptions, shows no blind eye to the powerful temptations of skepticism. Voltaire's attack on immortality is dreadful but "how plausible!" [80] The doctrine

77. *Idem*, pp. 287–288. The italics are mine.
78. *Idem*, p. 348. The italics are mine except for "is," which Newman italicized.
79. *Idem*, p. 331.
80. *Idem*, p. 107.

of eternal punishment is true but "terrible to the reason." [81] The existence of God is, of all points of faith, "encompassed with most difficulty"; and the usual arguments in proof of a God drawn from nature and society "do not warm me or enlighten me." [82] In fact, for Newman himself the vision of a world so full of suffering and evil, of misery and injustice, "seems simply to give the lie to that great truth." As with his confession of personal faults and errors, his recognition of the difficulties of faith could not but make him peculiarly sympathetic to the British public of the 1860's. [83]

So far, the apologetic methods described are more negative than positive. They remove suspicious and potential hostility by presenting Newman as an honest, fair-minded human being. But, in addition, other methods seek for positive attraction by drawing out what is charming in his personality or pathetic in his story.

There is, for example, the marked strain of modesty. "I am not setting myself up," he says, "as a pattern of good sense or of anything else." [84] He plays down his leadership of the Movement. "The true and primary author" was John Keble. And even after July, 1833, he modestly explains that "for myself, I was not the person to take the lead of a party; I never was, from first to last, more than *a* leading author of a school; nor did I ever wish to be anything else." [85] In this connection it is significant that Newman's "Autobiographical Memoir," written with no apolo-

81. *Idem,* p. 110.
82. *Idem,* pp. 332, 334, the latter of which is also the reference for the next quotation.
83. In this connection it is significant that John Morley, *Recollections* (1917, 2 vols.), I, 18, uses the *Apologia,* pp. 332–334, as an index to the spirit of the time and claims that Newman's passage was the "heart-piercing case that stood at hand."
84. *Apologia,* p. 131.
85. *Idem,* pp. 119, 159, respectively. The italics are mine.

getic intention, reveals by contrast a strain of egotism and conceit; and the implication that he toned down the *Apologia* is borne out by parallel passages. In the account of Whately, for example, the "Memoir" quotes his compliment that Newman "was the clearest-headed man he knew," and reprints his praise for Newman's contribution to the *Elements of Logic*. Both are omitted from the corresponding pages in the *Apologia*.[86] The notice of the Oriel election, barely mentioned in the latter and then only to illustrate his hero worship of Keble, appears in the "Memoir" replete with all the flattering details.[87]

Not that Newman excludes all praise of himself from the *Apologia*. That too would have been a tactical error. Compliments are introduced, not too often, carefully spaced, and modestly depreciated. In a quarterly for April, 1845, was "an exceedingly kind article" in which "the writer praised me in feeling and beautiful language far above my deserts." [88] Blanco White, after speaking "bitterly and unfairly of me" in his letters of 1833 (here omitted with the subtle implication that printing them would be as unfair to White as to Newman) changed his opinion later to high praise of "the amiable, the intellectual, the refined John Henry Newman." The praise, which is printed at length, is nicely introduced: "In 1839, when looking back, he uses terms of me, which it would be hardly modest in me to quote, were it not that what he says of me in praise is but part of a whole account of me." [89] Writ-

---

86. *Letters*, I, 105, 106; cf. *Apologia*, pp. 114–117. The "Memoir" was written in 1874 to supplement the brevity of the *Apologia* up to 1833; see *Letters*, I, 5.

87. *Letters*, I, 71–72; cf. *Apologia*, p. 119. For other examples in the "Memoir" of a strain of conceit not found in the *Apologia*, see *Letters*, I, 32, 33, 73, 74.

88. *Apologia*, p. 323.

89. *Idem*, pp. 149–150.

ing of his conversion, he prints some sentences from a letter of Charles Marriott's, a kind of testimonial to his loyalty to the Church of England and therefore important for the defence. "I quote them," says Newman disarmingly, "for the love which I bear him, and the value that I set on his good word"—which beautifully hides his real purpose behind a compliment and completely forestalls the appearance of egotism otherwise certain to arise.[90]

Still more winning than modesty is the impression of unselfish warmth and generosity which the last illustration suggests. Even for men with whom he was known to have quarreled there are expressions of respect, sometimes of love. He speaks of Hawkins and Whately with positive affection, and we do not question it, partly because the simplicity of style has the very air of sincerity I spoke of, partly because of the reference, without the least note of rancor, to disagreements he had with them both.[91] Had such disagreements been omitted, then for all who knew of them—and there were many—the expression of affection, standing alone, unqualified, would have been suspect. That was the negative advantage. The positive value of admitting old differences was the implied picture of a Newman whose friendship was broad and deep and forgiving enough to survive personal frictions without cherishing the slightest ill will (the suggestion of Christian forgiveness is not to be overlooked). Incidentally, it is worth noticing that Newman spoke more harshly both of Hawkins and of himself in a private note written in 1860. There he described the state of their relations from 1829 to 1845 as "a state of constant bickerings, of coldness, dryness, and donnishness on his part, and of provoking insubordination

90. *Idem,* p. 324.
91. *Idem,* pp. 111, 114–117.

and petulance on mine." [92] But, in an apologia, he could
not risk expressing such rancor toward another or such
damning criticism of himself.

If Newman could speak well of his enemies, it is not
surprising that he could write of his friends with an ardor
not the least mawkish or sentimental, and at times genu-
inely moving. Under the trials of 1841–45 he noted that
people thought he had "much to bear externally, disappointment, slander, &c." "No," he says at once, "I have
nothing to bear, but the anxiety which I feel for my friends'
anxiety for me, and their perplexity." [93] He would not
confide in J. W. Bowden, his "dear and old friend." "Why
should I unsettle that sweet calm tranquillity, when I had
nothing to offer him instead?" [94] And no one can forget
the superb peroration with which he offers his book to his
friends as a memorial of affection and gratitude:

And to you especially, dear AMBROSE ST. JOHN; whom
God gave me, when He took every one else away; who are
the link between my old life and my new; who have now for
twenty-one years been so devoted to me, so patient, so zealous,
so tender; who have let me lean so hard upon you; who have
watched me so narrowly; who have never thought of yourself,
if I was in question.

And in you I gather up and bear in memory those familiar
affectionate companions and counsellors, who in Oxford were
given to me, one after another, to be my daily solace and re-
lief; and all those others, of great name and high example,

92. This note is quoted in the article by Henry Tristram in *Revue Anglo-
Américaine*, XI (1933–34), 482. In passing, it may be noticed that in the
same note Newman says that since 1845 he has "had nothing but affectionate feelings for him [Hawkins]," which verifies the claim of affection
in the *Apologia*, p. 111.

93. *Apologia*, p. 317.

94. *Idem*, p. 316.

who were my thorough friends, and showed me true attachment in times long past.[95]

This, of course, shows Newman loved as well as loving, and elsewhere he says directly, "It was not I who sought friends, but friends who sought me. Never man had kinder or more indulgent friends than I have had." [96] Such passages reinforce those I mentioned earlier where he allows others to praise him. Also, they show him befriended in his hour of trial. He was not suspected, rejected, attacked by everybody. No, he had a few loyal and staunch friends who knew him well and stood by him. In that way these passages make more persuasive the last and most effective appeal of all, sympathy for the innocent and pathetic victim of persecution.

This appeal is handled with great tact. Either Newman makes no direct bid for sympathy, or if he does, he counteracts any suggestion of self-pity or self-centered concern by stressing his unselfish affection for others. In the former case, he invokes a principle dear to every Englishman, the principle of fair play, which at once wins support for anyone treated unfairly, and without his having to ask for it. It is thus an ideal technique for the apologist. In the discussion of Tract 90, for one example, Newman points out that "every creed has texts in its favour, and again texts which run counter to it." And then he continues with telling force:

. . . how had I done worse in Tract 90 than Anglicans, Wesleyans, and Calvinists did daily in their Sermons and their publications? how had I done worse, than the Evangelical party in their *ex animo* reception of the Services for Bap-

95. *Idem,* p. 372.
96. *Idem,* p. 117; cf. *idem,* p. 316. And see the brilliant rhetorical use Newman makes of friends' rallying around him which I point out below, p. 86.

tism and Visitation of the Sick? Why was I to be dishonest and
they immaculate? There was an occasion on which our Lord
gave an answer, which seemed to be appropriate to my own
case, when the tumult broke out against my Tract:—"He that
is without sin among you, let him first cast a stone at him." I
could have fancied that a sense of their own difficulties of interpretation would have persuaded the great party I have
mentioned to some prudence, or at least moderation, in opposing a teacher of an opposite school. But I suppose their
alarm and their anger overcame their sense of justice.[97]

After which, what reader does not assert his *own* sense of
justice—for *Newman!* The same technique is used with
even greater success in the account of the petty surveillance
and interference he was subjected to at Littlemore, for here
he can also appeal to a second principle equally dear to
the hearts of Englishmen. "Why may I not have that lib-
erty which all others are allowed?" "Am I alone, of Englishmen, not to have the privilege to go where I will, no
questions asked?" And so on, even to the sure-fire "I had
thought that an Englishman's house was his castle." [98]
Contrasted with such indirect methods for winning sympathy is the direct presentation of the "pathetic image."
It has already been seen in two passages quoted earlier:
that on the pain of ripping up old griefs ("See what Kingsley is putting me through"—though of course the actual
implication is a good deal more oblique and delicate) and
especially that on the final departure from Oxford.[99] I
have ascribed the latter to Newman's sense of the dramatic.
It was equally intended (and again we see that the book is a
single entity fusing apology and revelation) to end his
story with the pathetic picture of a kind, affectionate man,

97. *Apologia,* pp. 185–186.
98. *Idem,* pp. 269, 267.
99. *Idem,* pp. 191–192, 327.

heart-sick and lonely, leaving his old home forever. And to this is added very discreetly the image of persecution: "Trinity had never been unkind to me." But Oriel? the heads of the colleges? the Hebdomadal Board? Convocation?—every one of them, so wisely unmentioned, crowds into the reader's memory. And then the last pathetic touch: he has never seen Oxford since, except for the spires seen from the railway, with all its poignant connotations of banishment and exile. The force of Newman's persuasive rhetoric, which incidentally manages deftly to avoid, if only barely, the sentimental, can be further appreciated, if the reader desires, by turning back to the comparison of the passage with the account in his diary, quoted on an earlier page.[100] And we have, moreover, the evidence of one reader's reaction. Samuel Wilberforce, quoting the passage in his review, spoke of the "most touching words" which close this mournful story and gather up "an exceeding sadness."[101]

Perhaps the most subtle example of the pathetic image occurs in the closing paragraphs on Tract 90. Their very placing is skillful. Newman has just finished a full and clear statement of his case. He was not trying to Romanize the Church but simply to reassert those primitive doctrines which had once been in the English Church and which could be found, under a mass of ambiguities, in the Prayer-Book and the Articles. It was true, these doctrines were also Roman doctrines, but that was merely because Rome too had its roots in the Catholic and Apostolic Church. Now even if the reader suspects Newman's motive, he has to grant that the case is a good one. Newman might perfectly well have been doing precisely what he says he was doing—or he might not. But certainly he deserves a fair

100. Page 65.
101. *The Quarterly Review,* CXVI (1864), 558, 559.

hearing. If he were not to get it, if he should be condemned without trial, persecuted, slandered—how appalling! how unjust! That is the reader's state of mind as he reaches the conclusion, which must be quoted almost completely:

In the universal storm of indignation with which the Tract was received throughout the country on its appearance, I recognize much of real religious feeling, much of honest and true principle, much of straightforward ignorant common sense. In Oxford there was genuine feeling too; but there had been a smouldering stern energetic animosity, not at all unnatural, partly rational, against its author. A false step had been made; now was the time for action. . . .

I saw indeed clearly that my place in the Movement was lost; public confidence was at an end; my occupation was gone. It was simply an impossibility that I could say any thing henceforth to good effect, when I had been posted up by the marshal on the buttery hatch of every College of my University, after the manner of discommoned pastry-cooks, and when in every part of the country and every class of society, through every organ and occasion of opinion, in newspapers, in periodicals, at meetings, in pulpits, at dinner-tables, in coffee-rooms, in railway carriages, I was denounced as a traitor who had laid his train and was detected in the very act of firing it against the time-honoured Establishment. There were indeed men, besides my own immediate friends, men of name and position, who gallantly took my part, as Dr. Hook, Mr. Palmer, and Mr. Perceval: it must have been a grievous trial for themselves.[102]

In the face of such provocation, Newman's quiet restraint is instantly admirable. And under the circumstances, how just and fair of him to recognize that there *was* "real religious feeling" and "honest and true principle" against him, as well, no doubt (the reader is now ready on his part to be broad-minded), as some ignorant common sense. Then

102. *Apologia,* pp. 186–187.

the persecution: *this* man treated as a pastry cook, denounced as a traitor, *this* man whose case was at the worst highly debatable. And besides, a man with friends; and friends who stuck by him; and not simply personal friends but others who took his part and gallantly supported a lost cause; and they were no ordinary men, but men "of name and position." Then comes the last touch, the fine note of unselfish thoughtfulness: "it must have been a grievous trial *for themselves.*" It is irresistible. No wonder Newman won his case, hands down. For, as he knew so well, "men go by their sympathies, not by argument." [103]

The first pamphlet (Part I) closed with a personal character sketch. As we look back on it, at this point, we can see how constantly it has been in Newman's mind, for all the methods of apology come under one or another characteristic which he ascribes to himself:

Whatever judgment my readers may eventually form of me from these pages, I am confident that they will believe me in what I shall say in the course of them. I have no misgiving at all, that they will be ungenerous or harsh with a man who . . . has ever spoken too much rather than too little; who would have saved himself many a scrape, if he had been wise enough to hold his tongue; who has ever been fair to the doctrines and arguments of his opponents; who has never slurred over facts and reasonings which told against himself; . . . who has never shrunk from confessing a fault when he felt that he had committed one; who has ever consulted for others more than for himself; who has given up much that he loved and prized and could have retained, but that he loved honesty better than name, and Truth better than dear friends.[104]

"That," says Newman to the reader, "is what I really am. Read the evidence that follows and see if I don't prove it."

103. *Idem*, p. 230.
104. *Idem*, p. 82.

PART THREE

EVALUATION

IX DIFFICULTIES AND LIMITATIONS

No biography so concrete and human as the *Apologia* was ever so difficult to read. Most readers find much of it obscure, oblique, and indigestible. That is largely because Newman wrote for an audience which today hardly exists outside colleges and seminaries, and even there is small. In 1864 it was still possible, for one thing, to rely on touch-and-go references to recent events. If he remarked in passing that "in 1828 or 1827 I had voted in the minority, when the Petition to Parliament against the Catholic Claims was brought into Convocation," [1] he had no need to explain how the minority voted or what were the Catholic claims.

For another thing, he could use many a theological and ecclesiastical term without stopping to define it. The religious character of Victorian education and the great importance of the religious problem, together with the constant presence of religious controversy in books, periodicals, and newspapers, guaranteed Newman an audience able, as no audience would be today, to understand his terms, in both the literal and metaphorical sense of the word.[2] As a result, the general reader of 1864 would have met the Apostolic Succession, or Baptismal Regeneration, or Final Perseverance without turning a hair. He would have known an Evangelical or an Anglo-Catholic when he saw one, in life or in print. He did not have to be introduced to Whately and Hampden and Thomas Arnold: they were

1. *Apologia*, p. 117.
2. Cf. the evidence of Henry Sidgwick in 1861 (*Henry Sidgwick: A Memoir*, by A.S. and E.M.S. [1906], pp. 64–65): "A large portion of the laity now, though unqualified for abstruse theological investigations, are yet competent to hear and decide on theological arguments."

still well-known advocates of liberal doctrines that were common knowledge. So it was that Newman could say, abruptly, "For his [Dr. Whately's] special theological tenets I had no sympathy," [3] and pass on, confident that even so important a point would be quite clear to his reader. Indeed, in the whole passage on the Noetics, what does Newman emphasize but Catholic doctrines which were not in the least typical of liberal Protestantism in general or even of this group in particular? He stresses them because, in retrospect, they were seen to be what he permanently assimilated in those years. He had no fear, in 1864, that anyone would misunderstand. But today, taken with the absence of any clear statement at that point of characteristically liberal doctrines, a modern reader is not much to be blamed for failing to grasp the real influences which Newman met with in the Oriel common room. And failure here is serious, for the experience of liberal thought at first-hand and the resulting awareness of its tendency to wreck theology, if not religion itself, had much to do with his advance to Catholicism.

Though Newman did not realize that in our time politics would displace religion as the problem of the age, he did see clearly the rising tide of religious indifference; and therefore, had he sat down in leisurely fashion to write for posterity, he might have anticipated our difficulties. As it was, however, the book had to be written rapidly, under the greatest pressure, a new chapter a week from April twenty-first to June second.[4] All definitions, explanations, "background" material which could possibly be dispensed with had to be omitted.

All that may explain. Does it excuse? The answer, I think, is that here the question of excuse is beside the point.

3. *Apologia*, p. 116.
4. See Ward, *Life, II,* 18, 25.

Newman's reliance upon an extensive body of knowledge means that today, and no doubt in the future, he cannot expect to be widely read.[5] That is his limitation; but it is not an artistic limitation. To understand *Paradise Lost* demands, I suspect, as much background as to understand the *Apologia*. For both, no doubt, the audience today is fit, though few.

Newman's book, however, is limited in another way which does affect its artistic value. It is centered upon Newman's changing beliefs to the exclusion of everything else. His reply to an inquiry about why he did not deal with his undergraduate years shows that this was conscious and deliberate: "It is 'a history of my religious opinions,' and I had no change in them when I was an Undergraduate. It would have been officious and impertinent to have spoken of myself at that time, since it did not bear on my subject." [6] Indeed, the whole period down to 1833 (that is, Part III) is so briefly sketched that in 1874 Newman wrote his "Autobiographical Memoir" to cover "my life up to 1833, which, with the 'Apologia' from 1833, would finish my Protestant years." [7] As that indicates, the book stops at 1845, thereby omitting the period down to 1864 which he might have included. But there again the limitation is deliberate, and on the same theory. "From the time that I became a Catholic," he says at the opening of Part VII, "of course I have no further history of my religious opinions to narrate," because "I have had no changes to record." [8]

Not only does this focus exclude or abbreviate periods

5. A good annotated edition would do much, of course, to solve this difficulty but, incredible as it seems, no such edition exists. It is one of the major desiderata of Victorian scholarship.
6. Printed in Cross, *Newman*, p. 171.
7. *Letters*, I, 5.
8. *Apologia*, p. 331.

of his life, it rules out his non-religious interests as well. We have to read his letters or others of his books to appreciate his talent for music, his taste for classical antiquity, and his efforts to reform the tutorial work in the University; or to see him with his mother and sisters and realize what they meant to him. Indeed, even his religious life is inadequately presented because those sides of it not closely connected with matters of historical and dogmatic Christianity, and hence with his changing creeds, are only implied or at best mentioned in passing. We learn nothing, for example, of his preaching and its enormous influence. We scarcely perceive the deep and interrelated strains of moralism, mysticism, and piety which formed so much of his religious character, though there are a few indications of these: the child's imagination, the pages on the Alexandrine Platonists, a paragraph on "Catholic feelings" of mystery and devotion,[9] and more striking, because of its position and its contrast of style, the quotation from "Divine Calls" that follows the account of his Monophysite-Donatist reading:

What can this world offer comparable with that insight into spiritual things, that keen faith, that heavenly peace, that high sanctity, that everlasting righteousness, that hope of glory, which they have, who in sincerity love and follow our Lord Jesus Christ? Let us beg and pray Him day by day to reveal Himself to our souls more fully, to quicken our senses, to give us sight and hearing, taste and touch of the world to come; so to work within us, that we may sincerely say, "Thou shalt guide me with Thy counsel, and after that receive me with glory. Whom have I in heaven but Thee? and there is none upon earth that I desire in comparison of Thee. My flesh and my heart faileth, but God is the strength of my heart, and my portion for ever." [10]

9. *Idem*, pp. 105–107, 127–130, 262, respectively.
10. *Idem*, p. 214.

It is relevant to notice that this passage, weaving together the mystical, ethical, and devotional, is from one of the *Parochial and Plain Sermons;* and it is characteristic of their tone and substance. To turn from Newman's biography to those sermons preached through the very years described in the *Apologia* is to discover a new dimension. It is at once to end the distortion which the book does not exactly give and yet which it does not guard against— that of a man whose religion is bounded by historical and dogmatic considerations.

Plainly, then, both much of Newman's life and various segments of his taste and personality have been left out of the *Apologia* or too briefly mentioned for their importance to be realized. Yet we must not overstress the point. We must balance the loss of range and fullness against the gain in concentration. By excluding all which did not bear directly upon his ideas of religious truth (together, of course, with their concomitant emotional attitudes and reactions), Newman was able to achieve a powerful artistic unity. The *Apologia* as it stands carries an impact not to be attained in a wider and looser framework. And the unity is the unity of Newman's life from his first conversion in 1816 to his last in 1845. It is the central line. How did it happen that this man who started as an Evangelical lost his Calvinism, became an Anglo-Catholic, and then went to Rome? And in that process what and how was he thinking and feeling? That is the *Apologia*. And there is no question that such a rigid focus, like a strict adherence to classical unities, gains compelling attention.

We have not yet, however, come to the main issue or issues. In asking, "How good is the *Apologia?*" we may dismiss the difficulties of reading and balance the limitations of range against the intensity of vision. But there remain other considerations that are decisive. Taking it simply as it stands, we want to know two things, and they correspond, naturally enough, with the dual character of the book. So far as it is an apology, did Newman tell the truth? So far as it is a work of psychological analysis, did he reveal the inner movement of his mind? In both cases, of course, there is also the question of style, but my judgment on that has been given. Whether for defence or for revelation, Newman's writing in the *Apologia* seems to me of the highest order. Is he to be praised as highly for the truth of his account and the fullness of his self-analysis?

X DID NEWMAN TELL THE TRUTH?

BIOGRAPHY presents a special problem in judicial criticism. It has to meet a double standard of truth. As with all works of art, we ask if this life is true to, in the sense of corresponds with, life as we know it. Is this man a fantastic invention or is he a probable human being? Is his character an incredible combination of discrepancies or has it the integration of a consistent personality? That is one standard, and it is as applicable to Shakespeare's Macbeth as to Boswell's Johnson or, so to speak, to Newman's Newman.

But there is another standard for biography which works of imagination alone can almost ignore. This is "scientific" truth, or fidelity to what may be publicly verified. However human he may be, however unified his character, is this the man who actually lived? Did he do these things? and at that time? and feel as we are told he felt? In short, is this biography true, not merely to life but to one particular individual life? And in the case of an apology these questions naturally become insistent.

We should note that this double standard opens the way to a conflicting evaluation, since a given life might be judged artistically true but historically false.[11] For autobiography, however, such a conclusion is not so damaging as it is for biography, since the very fact that distortion occurs, together with such explanations for it as are usually implied, gives us, however obliquely or unintentionally, evidence of the first importance about the man's actual character.[12]

11. See, for example, the passage quoted from F. L. Cross, below, p. 97.
12. See Leslie Stephen, "Autobiography," *Hours in a Library* (1899 ed.,

At this point the critical problem is further complicated by another consideration. If we decide that a biographer has written a fine piece of fiction, we have then to ask if he did so consciously or unconsciously; that is, whether the distortion was the result of intention or of personal limitations in knowledge or intelligence. Indeed, in the case of autobiography, the positive value of distortion, mentioned in the last paragraph, cannot be determined until these further questions are answered. If the departure from truth is deliberate, out of self-protection or ambition, the charge of insincerity is fair. But the charge is not fair, of course, if it is not intended and is simply the result of faulty memory, limited self-knowledge, and so on. In the former case the distortion itself may be written off as so much fabrication, but in the latter it remains valuable as the author's own view of himself, however mistaken.

The very title of Newman's life raises all of these questions. "Apologia" suggests distortion, and consciously intended; and the suspicion is strengthened by our study of Newman's rhetoric of persuasion which has been shown so extensive and skillful as to be certainly conscious, especially in a writer so well studied in the arts of speech. We must not forget, however, that conscious rhetoric can be the medium of genuine experience and that under the circumstances it would be the most natural means for Newman to use in pleading for a "true" picture in place of Kingsley's "scarecrow . . . dressed up in my clothes." [13]

Certainly, when we examine his private letters and diaries, and his published works, and the comments of con-

---

3 vols.), III, 237, though I think he overstates the case: "It may be reckoned . . . as a special felicity that an autobiography, alone of all books, may be more valuable in proportion to the amount of misrepresentation which it contains . . . It is always curious to see how a man contrives to present a false testimonial to himself."

13. *Apologia,* p. 99.

temporary friends and enemies, we come away convinced that the picture is substantially true. Of course, it is shaded a little. Newman was not quite so modest or fair-minded as he painted himself. There is a strain of conceit in his "Memoir." [14] *The Difficulties Felt by Anglicans* is less tolerant than the *Apologia*. The tone with which he speaks elsewhere of his treatment by the British public can be irritable and querulous.[15] But such deviations are slight. And they are unavoidable. "I declare," he said, "I think it as rare a thing, candour in controversy, as to be a Saint." [16] The admirable thing is that under the circumstances Newman deviated so little from the truth. Fortunately, so far as his character went, his record was so good that honesty was, indeed, the best policy.

Was that also the policy employed in recounting his changes of belief and especially his final conversion? Or did the necessity of defence and the fact that he wrote as a Catholic alter the true perspective? F. L. Cross has recently answered "yes" to the second question in a passage worth quoting and examining at length, since it is the only serious charge ever made against the truth of the *Apologia*:

The *Apologia* is probably the greatest autobiography in the English language. But to grant this is not to pronounce any opinion as to its historical accuracy. Its claims as a work of literature rest upon a different set of considerations from successfulness as a mere chronicle. In fact, we believe it can be shown that the *Apologia* gives a distinctly misleading account

14. See above, pp. 78–79.
15. For example, in the essay on Keble, *Essays,* II, 424–427; in *Correspondence,* pp. 349–350, or a parallel passage in *Letters,* II, 449, where he speaks of "the atrocious lies—I can call them nothing else—which are circulated against myself," though he did call them something else in the *Apologia*.
16. *Letters,* II, 324.

of the chief motives which led to the event to justify which the work was written. For, whereas in the *Apologia* the predominating factors which led to Newman's conversion are represented as being intellectual in character, the course of events shows that the really powerful motives were of a psychological nature and developed out of the acute circumstances connected with the publication of Tract 90. Newman's temperament was far too distrustful of reason for him ever to have been led to such a radical change on primarily intellectual grounds.

In the *Apologia* there is a curious mixture of fiction and truth, of *Dichtung* and *Wahrheit*. In so far as the *Apologia* narrates the *doctrinal* considerations which had weighed with Newman,—and, of course, considerations of this character played their part,—it is exceptionally accurate . . . In matters of fact, serious errors cannot be detected in the *Apologia*. In so far as the representation is in error,—and we are convinced that it is fundamentally in error,—it is in the way the whole drama is staged.[17]

In short, the drama is staged to show an intellectual development from the summer of 1839 to October, 1845, leading Newman slowly but logically to Rome, whereas in matter of fact the real turning point, according to Cross, was in 1841 with the hostile reception of Tract 90. That was followed by a growing sense of isolation, rejection, and resentment, which finally led to conversion as an act of revenge. "The Church was disgusted with Newman; the only step open to him in retaliation was to disown the Church." [18]

In the first place, Cross's admission of accuracy in doctrinal considerations and in matters of fact is borne out on examination. Chapter and verse, in the letters, in ar-

17. *Newman,* pp. 132–133.
18. *Idem,* p. 143. That Newman was driven on to secession through resentment at the persecution of the liberals was long ago argued by Wilberforce, *The Quarterly Review,* CXVI (1864), 543–544, 555–556.

ticles, in books, confirm the *Apologia*. And close proof-reading of a dozen sources has shown Newman scrupulously faithful in his quotations. Where words are occasionally altered or sentences omitted, the reason is clearly relevance or clarity.

In the next place, what grounds are there for Cross's theory of resentment as the major cause of conversion? What are *his* sources that we should credit them sufficiently to question the truth of Newman's own account? He mentions two. The first is implied in the remark that Newman's temperament was far too distrustful of reason for him to be converted on intellectual grounds—namely, the epistemology of the *University Sermons* and *The Grammar of Assent*. But the second source, surprisingly enough, is the *Apologia*. Cross closes his case by saying: "That it was considerations of this character [isolation, resentment, and so on] which weighed primarily in determining Newman's secession is borne out by a careful study of the *Apologia*." [19] And so, after all, the book *does contain* what Cross considers a true picture, even though that is not the picture it *presents*. This, I think, is correct. There is abundant evidence in the book that (1) Newman was strongly influenced by "psychological" factors and (2) after Tract 90 he became increasingly bitter and resentful.

If the whole truth, then, is *in* the *Apologia*, Cross's earlier remark about truth and fiction seems much too hasty. Nevertheless, his main thesis is still intact. For, even if the corrective could be found in the *Apologia*, the staging could still be misleading. By emphasis and shaping, the final picture—though with the corrective, hardly fictitious—might still be out of focus. R. H. Hutton once spoke of the chasm between Newman's rational arguments and "the motive powers *he betrays to us*, and which he

19. Cross, *Newman*, p. 143.

ultimately perhaps recognized himself as the moving forces of his own mind." [20] And so we seem to reach this conclusion: that, although Newman exposed all of his emotional drives, he laid major emphasis upon logical arguments and thus gave an impression of himself which is not strictly true.

The term "emphasis" is ambiguous. I have already demonstrated the priority in number and importance of the passages describing "states of mind" over those that set down "methods of thought." Still, the latter do get what may be called major rhetorical emphasis. They are pointed directly at the conclusion and they are played up, whereas the former are usually left standing alone, their influence only to be deduced, when possible, by the slow and careful reader. Under the circumstances, some such result could have been predicted. Newman knew he had to explain his shifting beliefs in terms which the general reader would understand and accept. As he says, he had to show he came by his opinions "through intelligible processes of thought." [21] And what would they be? The illative sense jumping mysteriously from this association to that analogy, from an obscure memory to a blind instinct? By no means. The only processes of thought that would be, or would seem to be, intelligible to a wide audience would be the usual methods of logic. He would have to emphasize conventional arguments even though the truth be blurred. Newman was quite clear about this. He saw that the "difficulty of analyzing our more recondite feelings happily and convincingly" had an important influence upon the science of Christian evidences:

20. *The Spectator,* XXXVII (1864), 655. The italics are mine. Though the article is unsigned, see Ward, *Life,* II, 522, for proof of Hutton's authorship.
21. *Apologia,* p. 131 n.

Did Newman Tell the Truth?

Defenders of Christianity naturally select as reasons for belief, not the highest, the truest, the most sacred, the most intimately persuasive, but such as best admit of being exhibited in argument; and these are commonly not the real reasons.

Nay, they are led, for the same reason, to select such arguments as all will allow; that is, such as depend on principles which are a common measure to all minds.[22]

This does not mean that the arguments given are made up but simply that "almost all reasons formally adduced in moral inquiries, are rather specimens and symbols of the real grounds, than those grounds themselves. They do but approximate to a representation of the general character of the proof which the writer wishes to convey to another's mind."[23] I have not the slightest doubt that Newman would have adapted these passages to explain his overemphasis on logical proofs in the science of personal apologetics and to indicate their limitation (to what all will allow) even in their own intellectual sphere. Substitute "defenders of themselves" for "defenders of Christianity," reread the quotations, and observe how neatly they fit the *Apologia*.[24]

On the other hand, it is equally easy to understand why Newman failed to emphasize the psychological factors cited by Cross. Assuming they were true and that he was aware of them, and both assumptions are well grounded,[25]

22. *University Sermons*, p. 267.

23. *Idem*, pp. 271–272.

24. Indeed, as he was planning the book, Newman wrote to Church (Ward, *Life*, II, 21) that "argument . . . as such will not come in, though I must state the *general* grounds of my change." The italics are mine.

25. The evidence in the *Apologia* is cited below on p. 111, n. 47. For supporting passages, see *Letters*, II, 425, 435, 443, 455–456; *Correspondence*, pp. 348, 349–350; the important letter quoted in Ward, *Life*, I, 81–82; and the unmistakably personal close of the sermon on "The Parting of Friends," *Sermons on Subjects of the Day*, pp. 406–408.

nevertheless how could he be expected to come out in an apologia and say bluntly, "I left the English Church from resentment at the way I was treated after Tract 90. That was the deciding factor." Could we expect anyone, however honest, to say that under the circumstances?

The extraordinary thing, *under the circumstances,* is that Newman should have expressed his real feelings at all. And not once or twice, in out-of-the-way corners, but in the forefront, so that they are only slightly less emphatic than the logical arguments. This is what Cross seems to overlook. There are not two views of the conversion, Cross's true one and Newman's false one. There is one view, with a slight difference in stress.

Consider, in the first place, the weight given in the *Apologia* to Tract 90 and its reception. Structurally, the year 1841, and not 1839, is at the center of the book. Both Part IV (in spite of its misleading title) and Part V end with the crucial events of that year. And Part IV specifically closes with the almost fanatical outburst that followed the publication of Tract 90. Newman notes that the "smouldering stern energetic animosity" against him, ever since 1833, now at last broke forth; that he had "fallen into the hands of the Philistines"; that he was unprepared for such an outbreak and "startled at its violence." [26] And, as we have already noticed, he does not hesitate to express his sense of unjust and contemptible persecution.[27] Still further, only a few pages earlier occurs the following passage, doubly significant from the fact that it introduces the account of Tract 90:

So I went on for years, *up to 1841.* It was, in a human point of view, the happiest time of my life. I was truly at home. I had

26. *Apologia,* p. 186.
27. Above, p. 85.

in one of my volumes appropriated to myself the words of Bramhall, "Bees, by the instinct of nature, do love their hives, and birds their nests." I did not suppose that such sunshine would last, though I knew not what would be its termination. It was the time of plenty, and, during its seven years, I tried to lay up as much as I could for the dearth which was to follow it.[28]

Thus the staging of Part IV, far from being misleading, gives full value to the crucial reception of Tract 90 in 1841 and its effect on Newman.

However, Part V opens with the portentous announcement, "I am about to trace . . . the course of that great revolution of mind, which led me to leave my own home." [29] And this is followed by the slow, dramatic build-up, already described, from April to August, 1839, ending with his belief in the theory of the *Via Media* being "absolutely pulverized." This is certainly another picture, and just as certainly it has been colored by subsequent events. Had Newman never seceded, the summer of 1839 would have taken its rightful place as the period when he first clearly saw the weak side of his case—a weakness seen without secession by plenty of other Anglicans, and which would have so been seen, I believe, by Newman himself had it not been for 1841. Indeed, the text contains a partial corrective, since various remarks put the summer reading "in its place." By January, 1840, he can write to his intimate friend Bowden about Wiseman's article on the Donatists in the past tense—that it "made me for a while very uncomfortable." In the spring of that year he can buy ten acres of ground at Littlemore and begin planting, which, he says, "shows how little I had really the idea then of ever leaving the Anglican Church." And there is the explicit

28. *Apologia*, p. 174. The italics are mine.
29. *Idem*, p. 191.

statement that *up to the "publication of Tract 90 in February, 1841,"* though "not confident about my permanent adhesion to the Anglican creed, . . . I was in no actual perplexity or trouble of mind." [30]

Part V closes with the three blows, in the latter half of 1841, that broke Newman's allegiance to the English Church. The first and third are doctrinal but the second is squarely psychological:

> The Bishops one after another began to charge against me. It was a formal, determinate movement. This was the real "understanding;" that, on which I had acted on occasion of Tract 90, had come to nought. I think the words, which had then been used to me, were, that "perhaps two or three of them might think it necessary to say something in their charges;" but by this time they had tided over the difficulty of the Tract, and there was no one to enforce the "understanding." They went on in this way, directing charges at me, for three whole years. I recognized it as a condemnation; it was the only one that was in their power. At first I intended to protest; but I gave up the thought in despair.[31]

To feel the tension here we must know the background. The understanding on which Newman had acted was that, if he did not defend Tract 90, the bishops would not condemn it.[32] Thus, the bitter sense of having been tricked is added to the distress we can hear in the word "condemnation" when we also remember that for Newman the voice of his bishop was *jure divino:* "My own Bishop was my Pope." [33]

Finally, throughout the last chapter (that is, Part VI, the last chapter of the narrative, from 1841 to 1845) we

30. *Idem,* pp. 226, 228, 232, respectively. The italics are mine.
31. *Idem,* pp. 235–236.
32. See *idem,* pp. 187–188.
33. *Idem,* p. 152; and cf. *idem,* pp. 175, 176, 204, 280.

find the recurrent note of isolation and bitterness. He mentions, without denial, the "idea afloat that my retirement from the Anglican Church was owing to the feeling that I had so been thrust aside, without any one's taking my part." [34] There is the telling remark at the very close: "Trinity had never been unkind to me." [35] There is the revealing letter written to Manning in October, 1843, which must be quoted at length. Newman is speaking of the "feelings and reasons" which led him to resign St. Mary's:

The nearest approach I can give to a general account of them is to say, that it has been caused by the general repudiation of the view, contained in No. 90, on the part of the Church. I could not stand against such an unanimous expression of opinion from the Bishops, supported, as it has been, by the concurrence, or at least silence, of all classes in the Church, lay and clerical. If there ever was a case, in which an individual teacher has been put aside and virtually put away by a community, mine is one. No decency has been observed in the attacks upon me from authority; no protests have been offered against them. It is felt,—I am far from denying, justly felt,— that I am a foreign material, and cannot assimilate with the Church of England.

Even my own Bishop has said that my mode of interpreting the Articles makes them mean *any thing or nothing*. When I heard this delivered, I did not believe my ears. I denied to others that it was said . . . Out came the charge, and the words could not be mistaken. This astonished me the more,

34. *Idem,* p. 323. It is fair to add, however, that on p. 317 he says that people are mistaken who think he has "much to bear externally, disappointment, slander, &c." Yet, plainly (see *Correspondence,* p. 348), Keble and other close friends were so certain that Newman was mainly suffering from feeling "solitary, or, as it were, cast out" that they were at pains to convince him of hundreds, not to say thousands, of people who loved him and honored him.

35. *Apologia,* p. 327.

because I published that Letter to him, (how unwillingly you know,) on the understanding that *I* was to deliver his judgment on No. 90 *instead* of him.[36]

What I would urge here is the primary status given the sense of injustice and persecution, even to the point of feeling hounded from the Church, with the concurrent emotions of anger and resentment. The theological argument, which follows in the next paragraph, comes in a poor second and almost like a rationale of the previous attitude. It would be more accurate, however, to say that these psychological factors provided the necessary impetus to carry Newman's intellectual conclusions from theory into action. And that is clearly implied by the confession which is quoted from a letter of November, 1844, only a few pages before the end:

The expression of opinion, and the latent and habitual feeling about me, which is on every side and among all parties, has great force. I insist upon it, because I have a great dread of going by my feelings, lest they should mislead me. By one's sense of duty one must go; but external facts support one in doing so.[37]

To bring together the passages cited on my last few pages is, of course, to produce a picture which is not to be found when they are returned to their scattered places in the book and become subordinate to Newman's emphasis upon a series of logical probabilities. Yet the emotional factors are clearly portrayed, and the picture we do get from the *Apologia* is not, I think, very much out of focus.

36. *Idem,* pp. 311–312. The italics are Newman's.
37. *Idem,* p. 321.

XI   HOW GOOD IS NEWMAN'S SELF-ANALYSIS?

Those who place the *Apologia* among the great autobiographies of the world, or call it the greatest in English, do so because they think it a superb work of psychological analysis. This was its praise from the start. In his review of 1864 Wilberforce found it "an absolute revealing of the hidden life in its acting, and its processes," and Dr. Irons wrote that "as a specimen of mental analysis, extended over a whole lifetime, the 'Apologia' is probably without a rival. St. Augustine's Confessions are a purely religious retrospect; Rousseau's are philosophical; Dr. Newman's psychological." [38] Such statements, however, have little meaning because the terms are too broad. If by mental analysis we mean a clear and ordered explanation of how these arguments and those facts, of how long-established prejudices and the emotions of the moment, all combined to lead a man forward through a series of actions and beliefs, then the *Apologia* can hardly claim, I think, to be psychological biography of a high order. Have we full and satisfactory motivation for a single turning point in his thought? For his abandoning the Evangelicals? or later, the Noetics? or for his adoption of Anglo-Catholicism? or even for his Roman conversion?

There are, of course, the direct arguments or, as Newman calls them, "methods of thought." There are also, at greater length, those "particular states of mind" which so materially influenced his reasoning. But, as I have shown, Newman rarely points out the crucial effects of the latter;

38. *The Quarterly Review,* CXVI (1864), 529; and, for Irons, Ward, *Life,* II, 34.

and, though sometimes we can deduce what they were, often we are uncertain or completely baffled. It is true that nothing seems omitted. We do not doubt that these were, indeed, the facts and the arguments and the emotional drives that determined this belief or that action. We are certain that influences sufficient to explain what happened are always there before us. And yet they are never clearly or fully arranged and related, nor their varying impacts assessed. Everything seems ready for synthesis, but the synthesis is never made.

Why that was so I have already sought to explain, by reference to both Newman's temperament and his theories of analysis.[39] Here I am only concerned with the fact, and the fact is damaging. The *Apologia* simply does not disclose "a hidden life in its acting and its processes."

And yet the hidden life is there, though not much of its acting and processes. An alternate remark of Wilberforce's lays the stress at the right place:

As an autobiography, in the highest sense of that word, as the portraiture, that is, and record of what the man was, . . . it is eminently dramatic.[40]

This recalls Newman's own phrasing, in his earliest comment on autobiography, about "delineating, or, as it were, painting what the mind sees and feels" [41]—*what* rather than *why*. And later, as he was planning the *Apologia*, he said, "I want to state the stages in my change and the impediments which kept me from going faster. Argument, I think, as such will not come in,—though I must state the general grounds of my change." [42] The stages, the suc-

39. Above, pp. 29–34.
40. *The Quarterly Review,* CXVI (1864), 528.
41. *University Sermons,* p. 263.
42. Ward, *Life,* II, 21.

cessive states of mind—that is primary, though he must add the *general* grounds of his reasoning. These remarks point the direction of Newman's biographical art. Though by no means ignored, the presentation of motives is neither sharp nor subtle; but in its place we have a remarkable revelation of personality.

This thesis has been supported and illustrated above, but, because it bears so closely upon the quality and calibre of the *Apologia*, a further illustration, pointed to the issue, will, I am sure, be valuable. I take Part VI on the period from 1841 to the actual conversion in 1845.

Judged as a rational account of Newman's final steps, the chapter is confused and disorganized. We do not see any progress. The conflicting arguments or conflicting attitudes are not balanced, nor the pros and cons compared or given their relative weight. The fact is that Newman never accounted to his own satisfaction, let alone to ours, for what happened in those crucial years. In November, 1844, writing of his Roman intentions to Keble, he confessed:

You must not suppose, I am fancying that I know *why* or on *what*, on what *motive*, I am acting. I cannot. I do not feel love, or faith. I feel myself very unreal. I can only say negatively, what I think does *not* influence me. But I cannot analyse my mind, and, I suppose, should do no good if I tried.[43]

No doubt this was written in a moment of extreme weakness (his spirits are plainly at a low ebb), and yet many other remarks, if less explicit, imply the same uncertainty of motive. When in May, 1843, he wrote Keble the "shocking" letter breaking the news of his drift toward Rome, he confessed he really could not say "whether I am stating my existing feelings, motives, and views fairly, and whether

43. *Correspondence*, p. 352.

my memory will not play me false. I cannot hope but I shall seem inconsistent to you—and whether I am or have been I cannot say. I will but observe that it is very difficult to realize one's own views in certain cases, *at the time* of acting." [44] And it proved just as difficult later. Part V opens: "And now that I am about to trace, *as far as I can*, the course of that great revolution of mind, which led me to leave my own home." [45] And just below he explains that the "perplexity and dismay" of these years made him even less able than usual to grasp the influences acting upon him.

Small wonder that when Newman comes to Part VI he feels it necessary to prefix a kind of apology for its incoherence. These were the years, he explains, when he was on his deathbed, as regards the Anglican Church, "and when the sick man neither cares nor is able to record the stages of his malady." In consequence his narrative must be in great measure documentary, as he cannot rely on his memory "except for definite particulars." He has some notes, though "no strictly personal or continuous memoranda." [46]

And yet, if there are no stages and no continuous narrative, there are the definite particulars—and they are used with great effect. If the motivation is obscure (I do not say it is altogether absent, but only that at best it must be reconstructed by the reader, as, for example, in such a way as was sketched out in the previous section), nevertheless the man himself is vividly and sharply revealed.

Newman is seen caught between conflicting forces that center not on Rome but on Oxford and all that it symbolized. He is driven in anger and revulsion toward flight,

44. *Idem*, p. 218.
45. *Apologia*, p. 191. The italics are mine.
46. All quotations are in *idem*, p. 245.

and yet at the same timě checked by fear of the consequences and held back by life-long habit and attachment. On the one hand, we see his distress over the hostile reception of Tract 90; his growing resentment at the bishops as they kept charging against him, and still more at the London newspapers and Oxford spies who broke in upon his privacy at Littlemore; the bitterness over whispered insinuations, once even by a bishop, that he was already in the pay of Rome; the protest that he was *not* acting out of irritation or disappointment reiterated until it implies the opposite; the sick awareness of old friends and acquaintances shrinking away from him as if he were tainted; and, above all, the desperate sense of isolation and loneliness, with the feeling of having been thrust aside "without any one's taking my part." [47] Is not all this brilliantly conveyed? And with equal sharpness we feel the counter emotions which delayed and so long paralyzed his decision: the painful prospect of a liberal triumph over his conversion; the haunting fear that he was under some great delusion; the passionate love of Oxford, with the deep inner need of holding fast to the old friends, the old affections.[48]

It is true enough that Newman never formally balances these states of mind or points out the crucial bearing of the former upon his final action. Which is only to say again that in the analysis of motive the *Apologia* is not very successful. Yet such an admission is less detrimental, I

47. For his distress about Tract 90, see *idem,* p. 186; for the bishops charging against him, *idem,* pp. 192, 235–236, 267, 299–300, 305, 311–312; for newspapers and spies, *idem,* pp. 266–267; for the insinuations of treachery, *idem,* pp. 269, 271–272; for his protesting rather too much, *idem,* pp. 312 (l. 24), 317 (l. 6), 319 (l. 31), 322 (l. 10); for friends shrinking away, *idem,* pp. 260, 261, 372; for the sense of isolation, *idem,* pp. 323, 327.

48. *Idem,* pp. 296; 318, 320 (and cf. *idem,* 215, earlier); 174, 191, 316–317, 319–320, 323, 327, 372, respectively.

think, than we might suppose. One recalls T. S. Eliot's well-known passage on the artistic handling of character: "What the creator of character needs is not so much knowledge of motives as keen sensibility; the dramatist need not understand people; but he must be exceptionally aware of them." [49] This seems to me precisely the case of Newman, even down to the term "dramatist." He could not distinguish and arrange and relate his motives into a consistent pattern, but he was exceptionally aware of himself. And for our part, we come away with a vivid and consistent sense of personality. *Why* he did this or did that may be doubtful, and often is, but we never doubt that *this* man would have acted in precisely *that* way. This conception of biography, so easily undervalued by an age of scientific analysis, has perhaps never been better stated than by Newman himself when he explained what he meant by a "Life":

I mean a narrative which impresses the reader with the idea of moral unity, identity, growth, continuity, personality, . . . of the presence of one active principle of thought, one individual character flowing on and into the various matters which he discusses, and the different transactions in which he mixes. [50]

49. From the essay on "Philip Massinger" (1920), in *Selected Essays, 1917–1932* (London, 1932), p. 212.
50. *Historical Sketches*, II, 227.

INDEX OF PROPER NAMES

Note: Articles and books, unless anonymous, are indexed under the author's name.

[113]